THE KEY—English Language Arts 3

THE KEY consists of the following sections:

KEY Tips for Being Successful at School gives examples of study and review strategies. It includes information about learning styles, study schedules, and note taking for test preparation.

Class Focus includes a unit on each area of the curriculum. Units are divided into sections, each focusing on one of the specific expectations, or main ideas, that students must learn about in that unit. Examples, definitions, and visuals help to explain each main idea. Practice questions on the main ideas are also included. At the end of each unit is a test on the important ideas covered. The practice questions and unit tests help students identify areas they know and those they need to study more. They can also be used as preparation for tests and quizzes. Most questions are of average difficulty, though some are easy and some are hard. Each unit is prefaced by a **Table of Correlations**, which correlates questions in the unit (and in the practice tests at the end of the book) to the specific curriculum expectations. Answers and solutions are found at the end of each unit.

KEY Strategies for Success on Tests helps students get ready for tests. It shows students different types of questions they might see, word clues to look for when reading them, and hints for answering them.

Practice Tests includes one to three tests based on the entire course. They are very similar to the format and level of difficulty that students may encounter on final tests. In some regions, these tests may be reprinted versions of official tests, or reflect the same difficulty levels and formats as official versions. This gives students the chance to practice using real-world examples. Answers and complete solutions are provided at the end of the section.

For the complete curriculum document (including specific expectations along with examples and sample problems), visit http://education.alberta.ca/teachers/core.aspx

THE KEY Study Guides are available for many courses. Check www.castlerockresearch.com for a complete listing of books available for your area.

For information about any of our resources or services, please call Castle Rock Research at 780.448.9619 or visit our website at http://www.castlerockresearch.com.

At Castle Rock Research, we strive to produce an error-free resource. If you should find an error, please contact us so that future editions can be corrected.

TABLE OF CONTENTS

NOTES

THE KEY
STUDENT STUDY GUIDE

English Language Arts 3

THE KEY student study guide is designed to help students achieve success in school. The content in each study guide is 100% curriculum aligned and serves as an excellent source of material for review and practice. To create this book, teachers, curriculum specialists, and assessment experts have worked closely to develop the instructional pieces that explain each of the key concepts for the course. The practice questions and sample tests have detailed solutions that show problem-solving methods, highlight concepts that are likely to be tested, and point out potential sources of errors. **THE KEY** is a complete guide to be used by students throughout the school year for reviewing and understanding course content, and to prepare for assessments.

Rao, Gautam, 1961 –
THE KEY – English Language Arts 3
ISBN: 978-1-77044-437-9

1.   English – Juvenile Literature. I. Title

Published by
Castle Rock Research Corp.
2000 First & Jasper
10065 Jasper Avenue
Edmonton, AB T5J 3B1

10 9 8 7 6 5 4

Publisher
Gautam Rao

Contributors
Tony d'Apice
Brigitta Braden
Erin Kubinec
Sally McIntosh
Christine Nehring
Lois Westerlund

CASTLE ROCK
RESEARCH CORP

Dedicated to the memory of Dr. V. S. Rao

KEY Tips for Being Successful at School

NOTES

KEY TIPS FOR BEING SUCCESSFUL AT SCHOOL

KEY FACTORS CONTRIBUTING TO SCHOOL SUCCESS

In addition to learning the content of your courses, there are some other things that you can do to help you do your best at school. You can try some of the following strategies:

- **Keep a positive attitude**: Always reflect on what you can already do and what you already know.

- **Be prepared to learn**: Have the necessary pencils, pens, notebooks, and other required materials for participating in class ready.

- **Complete all of your assignments**: Do your best to finish all of your assignments. Even if you know the material well, practice will reinforce your knowledge. If an assignment or question is difficult for you, work through it as far as you can so that your teacher can see exactly where you are having difficulty.

- **Set small goals for yourself when you are learning new material**: For example, when learning the parts of speech, do not try to learn everything in one night. Work on only one part or section each study session. When you have memorized one particular part of speech and understand it, move on to another one. Continue this process until you have memorized and learned all the parts of speech.

- **Review your classroom work regularly at home**: Review to make sure you understand the material you learned in class.

- **Ask your teacher for help**: Your teacher will help you if you do not understand something or if you are having a difficult time completing your assignments.

- **Get plenty of rest and exercise**: Concentrating in class is hard work. It is important to be well-rested and have time to relax and socialize with your friends. This helps you keep a positive attitude about your schoolwork.

- **Eat healthy meals**: A balanced diet keeps you healthy and gives you the energy you need for studying at school and at home.

HOW TO FIND YOUR LEARNING STYLE

Every student learns differently. The manner in which you learn best is called your learning style. By knowing your learning style, you can increase your success at school. Most students use a combination of learning styles. Do you know what type of learner you are? Read the following descriptions. Which of these common learning styles do you use most often?

- Do you need to say things out loud? You may learn best by saying, hearing, and seeing words. You are probably really good at memorizing things such as dates, places, names, and facts. You may need to write down the steps in a process, a formula, or the actions that lead up to a significant event, and then say them out loud.

- Do you need to read or see things? You may learn best by looking at and working with pictures. You are probably really good at puzzles, imagining things, and reading maps and charts. You may need to use strategies like mind mapping and webbing to organize your information and study notes.

- Do you need to draw or write things down? You may learn best by touching, moving, and figuring things out using manipulatives. You are probably really good at physical activities and learning through movement. You may need to draw your finger over a diagram to remember it, tap out the steps needed to solve a problem, or feel yourself writing or typing a formula.

SCHEDULING STUDY TIME

You should review your class notes regularly to ensure that you have a clear understanding of all the new material you learned. Reviewing your lessons on a regular basis helps you to learn and remember ideas and concepts. It also reduces the quantity of material that you need to study prior to a test. Establishing a study schedule will help you to make the best use of your time.

• Regardless of the type of study schedule you use, you may want to consider the following suggestions to maximize your study time and effort:

• Organize your work so that you begin with the most challenging material first.

• Divide the subject's content into small, manageable chunks.

• Alternate regularly between your different subjects and types of study activities in order to maintain your interest and motivation.

• Make a daily list with headings like "Must Do," "Should Do," and "Could Do."

• Begin each study session by quickly reviewing what you studied the day before.

• Maintain your usual routine of eating, sleeping, and exercising to help you concentrate better for extended periods of time.

CREATING STUDY NOTES

MIND-MAPPING OR WEBBING

Use the key words, ideas, or concepts from your class notes to create a mind map or web, which is a diagram or visual representation of the given information. A mind map or web is sometimes referred to as a knowledge map. Use the following steps to create a mind map or web:

1. Write the key word, concept, theory, or formula in the centre of your page.

2. Write down related facts, ideas, events, and information, and link them to the central concept with lines.

3. Use coloured markers, underlining, or symbols to emphasize things such as relationships, timelines, and important information.

The following mind map is an example of one that could help you develop an essay:

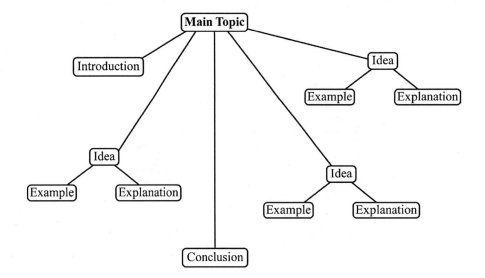

INDEX CARDS

To use index cards while studying, follow these steps:

1. Write a key word or question on one side of an index card.

2. On the reverse side, write the definition of the word, answer to the question, or any other important information that you want to remember.

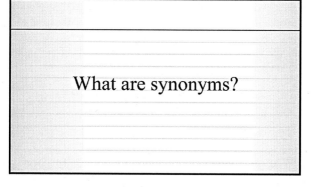

What are synonyms?

What are synonyms?
Synonyms are words that
have the same or almost the
same meaning.

For example, "coarse"
is a synonym for "rough"

SYMBOLS AND STICKY NOTES—IDENTIFYING IMPORTANT INFORMATION

Use symbols to mark your class notes. For example, an exclamation mark (!) might be used to point out something that must be learned well because it is a very important idea. A question mark (?) may highlight something you are not certain about, and a diamond (◊) or asterisk (*) could highlight interesting information that you want to remember. Sticky notes are useful in the following situations:

• Use sticky notes when you are not allowed to put marks in books.

• Use sticky notes to mark a page in a book that contains an important diagram, formula, explanation, or other information.

• Use sticky notes to mark important facts in research books.

MEMORIZATION TECHNIQUES

The following techniques can help you when you need to memorize something:

- **Association** relates new learning to something you already know. For example, to remember the spelling difference between dessert and desert, recall that the word *sand* has only one *s*. So, because there is sand in a desert, the word *desert* has only one *s*.

- **Mnemonic** devices are sentences that you create to remember a list or group of items. For example, the first letter of each word in the phrase "**E**very **G**ood **B**oy **D**eserves **F**udge" helps you to remember the names of the lines on the treble-clef staff (E, G, B, D, and F) in music.

- **Acronyms** are words that are formed from the first letters or parts of the words in a group. For example, RADAR is actually an acronym for Radio Detecting and Ranging, and MASH is an acronym for Mobile Army Surgical Hospital. HOMES helps you to remember the names of the five Great Lakes (Huron, Ontario, Michigan, Erie, and Superior).

- **Visualizing** requires you to use your mind's eye to "see" a chart, list, map, diagram, or sentence as it is in your textbook or notes, on the chalkboard or computer screen, or in a display.

- **Initialisms** are abbreviations that are formed from the first letters or parts of the words in a group. Unlike acronyms, an initialism cannot be pronounced as a word itself. For example, BEDMAS is an initialism for the order of operations in math (Brackets, Exponents, Divide, Multiply, Add, Subtract).

KEY STRATEGIES FOR REVIEWING

Reviewing textbook material, class notes, and handouts should be an ongoing activity. Spending time reviewing becomes more critical when you are preparing for a test. You may find some of the following review strategies useful when studying during your scheduled study time:

- Before reading a selection, preview it by noting the headings, charts, graphs, and chapter questions.

- Before reviewing a unit, note the headings, charts, graphs, and chapter questions.

- Highlight key concepts, vocabulary, definitions, and formulas.

- Skim the paragraph, and note the key words, phrases, and information.

- Carefully read over each step in a procedure.

- Draw a picture or diagram to help make the concept clearer.

KEY STRATEGIES FOR SUCCESS: A CHECKLIST

Reviewing is a huge part of doing well at school and preparing for tests. Here is a checklist for you to keep track of how many suggested strategies for success you are using. Read each question, and put a check mark (✓) in the correct column. Look at the questions where you have checked the "No" column. Think about how you might try using some of these strategies to help you do your best at school.

KEY Strategies for Success	Yes	No
Do you attend school regularly?		
Do you know your personal learning style—how you learn best?		
Do you spend 15 to 30 minutes a day reviewing your notes?		
Do you study in a quiet place at home?		
Do you clearly mark the most important ideas in your study notes?		
Do you use sticky notes to mark texts and research books?		
Do you practise answering multiple-choice and written-response questions?		
Do you ask your teacher for help when you need it?		
Are you maintaining a healthy diet and sleep routine?		
Are you participating in regular physical activity?		

Reading

TABLE OF CORRELATIONS

General Outcome	Specific Outcome	Practice Questions	Unit Test
Students are expected to ...			
2.1 Use strategies and cues	2.1.1.2 identify the different ways in which oral, print and other media texts, such as stories, textbooks, letters, pictionaries and junior dictionaries, are organized		7
	2.1.2.1 use grammatical knowledge to predict words and sentence structures when reading narrative and expository materials	17, 26	12
	2.1.2.2 apply a variety of strategies, such as setting a purpose, confirming predictions, making inferences and drawing conclusions	1, 12, 15, 28, 30, 37, 51	1, 3, 8
	2.1.2.3 identify the main idea or topic and supporting details in simple narrative and expository passages	34, 41, 42, 45	
	2.1.2.4 extend sight vocabulary to include predictable phrases and words related to language use	8, 10	20, 21, 27
	2.1.2.6 monitor and confirm meaning by rereading when necessary, and by applying knowledge of pragmatic, semantic, syntactic and graphophonic cueing systems	9, 13, 20, 24, 29, 50	2, 10, 13, 22
	2.1.3.1 use headings, paragraphs, punctuation and quotation marks to assist with constructing and confirming meaning	14, 52	
	2.1.4.1 apply phonic rules and generalizations competently and confidently to read unfamiliar words in context.	3, 27	6
	2.1.4.2 apply word analysis strategies to segment words into parts or syllables, when reading unfamiliar words in context	11, 19, 25, 46	4
	2.1.4.3 associate sounds with an increasing number of vowel combinations, consonant blends and digraphs, and letter clusters to read unfamiliar words in context	43, 44	
	2.1.5.1 put words in alphabetical order by first and second letter	16, 48	5

2.2 Respond to texts	2.2.1.1 choose a variety or oral, print and other media texts for shared and independent listening, reading and viewing experiences, using texts from a variety of cultural traditions and genres, such as nonfiction, chapter books, illustrated storybooks, drum dances, fables, CDROM programs and plays		16, 17
	2.2.1.3 identify types of literature, such as humour, poetry, adventure and fairy tales, and describe favourites		15
	2.2.2.2 summarize the main idea of individual oral, print and other media texts	6, 53	18, 19
	2.2.2.4 make inferences about character's actions or feelings	18, 38, 54	11, 24
	2.2.3.2 identify how authors use comparisons, and explain how they create mental images	22, 31	
2.3 Understand forms, elements and techniques	2.3.1.1 identify distinguishing features of a variety of oral, print and other media texts	2	
	2.3.1.2 discuss ways that visual images convey meaning in print and other media texts	4	
	2.3.2.1 include events, setting and characters when summarizing or retelling oral, print or other media texts	5, 35, 47	
	2.3.2.2 describe the main characters in terms of who they are, their actions in the story and their relations with other characters	23, 36	
	2.3.2.3 identify ways that messages are enhanced in oral, print and other media texts by the use of specific techniques	49	

3.1 Plan and focus	3.1.1.2 identify facts and opinions, main ideas and details in oral, print and other media texts	7	
3.2 Select and process	3.2.2.1 use text features, such as titles, pictures, heading, labels, diagrams and dictionary guide words to access information		26
	3.2.2.2 locate answers to questions and extract appropriate and significant information from oral, print and other media texts	33, 37, 39, 40	23, 25
3.3 Organize, record and evaluate	3.3.1.1 organize ideas using a variety of strategies, such as clustering, categorizing and sequencing		14
4.2 Attend to conventions	4.2.3.2 use exclamation marks, appropriately, as end punctuation in own writing	21	
	4.2.3.4 identify commas, end punctuation, apostrophes and quotation marks when reading, and use them to assist comprehension		9

READING FOR UNDERSTANDING

2.1.2.2   *Apply a variety of strategies, such as setting a purpose, confirming predictions, making inferences, and drawing conclusions*

HELPFUL IDEAS FOR READING

People have their own ways they like to read. If you are someone who likes to simply start at the first word and read straight through to the end, you may find some of the following ideas helpful. When you first try them, you might find that it takes you a little longer to read. With practice, you will probably find that you will get faster, but, more importantly, you will understand and remember more of what you read.

Asking questions will help you become an active, thoughtful, reflective, and skilled reader. Here are some questions to ask **before**, **during**, and **after** reading a piece of text.

Before Reading

- Why am I reading this?
- What will I be doing with the information I read?
- What do I already know about the topic?
- What do I think I will learn?
- What are my predictions?
- What reading strategies should I use to read this text?
- How is the text organized?
- What questions do I have before reading this text?

During Reading

- Am I meeting the purpose I set for reading this?
- Am I making sense of what I am reading?
- Do I understand what I am reading?
- Do I have a clear picture in my mind's eye?
- Is what I am reading what I expected?
- Are some parts different or similar to my predictions?

After Reading

- Do I need to re-read any parts that were difficult?
- Did I learn what I wanted to learn?
- What new information did I learn, and how does it fit into my background knowledge?
- What else do I still need to know about the topic?
- What are my thoughts about what I have read?
- Do I agree or disagree? Why?
- Do I like what I have read? Why or why not?

WHY WE READ

Why do we read? Think of all the different reasons people read books, websites, maps, recipes, dictionaries, magazines and so on. Sometimes we read just for fun. Sometimes we read to learn something new. Sometimes to answer questions we have. Sometimes to find out what is going on in the world. What other reasons can you think of? Why would you read a street sign? Why would you read the instructions on a test? Why would you read an adventure novel?

These reasons give you a **purpose** for reading. It is helpful to know your purpose or reason before choosing your reading material and starting to read. If your reason for reading is to be amused, you will choose a book by an author you know is funny, such as Farley Mowatt or Dav Pilkey. If your reason for reading is to learn how to fix the chain on your bike, you will probably not read the whole book on bike repair, but rather flip to the section on fixing the chain. These are examples of how knowing your reading purpose helps you to select and read effectively.

PREDICTIONS

When you make a prediction, you guess what you will learn or what will happen in the text. Things that can help you make predictions are headings of chapters or sections, and pictures and diagrams. You can also read the first sentences of paragraphs or sections, and look for important words. This helps you get a good idea of what the writing will be about. It also helps you understand the text more fully when you actually read it. Ask yourself these questions before reading to help predict what the text will be about:

1. Do the title, headings, and illustrations hint at what the text is about? Do they remind you of anything you already know about the topic?
2. As you read some of the first sentences under the headings, can you guess at what the rest of the paragraphs might be about?
3. Do any words stand out or hint at what the text is about?

As you are reading the text, notice if your predictions are correct or if you need to change them. Ask yourself these questions during and after reading to confirm if your predictions are correct:

1. Is what I am reading what I expected?
2. Are some parts different or similar to my predictions?
3. Do I need to reread any parts to check my predictions?

MAKING INFERENCES AND DRAWING CONCLUSIONS

When you read, you make decisions or get ideas about characters and events that are in the story without being told directly. This is called inferring.
You make inferences by carefully reading the important ideas in the story and deciding why something happens. When one action causes another action to occur, we say that there has been a "cause and effect." Sometimes, you will realize that something that happens in a story was caused by an action that happened earlier in the story. Other times, when you read that a particular action occurs in a story (a cause), you can infer what will happen next (the effect). Looking for "cause-and-effect" relationships in stories will also help you to make **predictions** (guesses) and draw **conclusions** (decisions) to help you understand the whole story better.

> ### *from* BELLE'S JOURNEY
>
> Every Saturday on the great wide prairie, Molly rode her brown mare Belle to piano lessons. Eight miles to the piano teacher's house and eight miles home.
>
> On hot summer days they rode under a high yellow sun and a blue sky. In winter they trudged along the trails beneath grey skies and a low pale sun that gave no warmth.
>
> Molly rode bareback, as there was no money for a saddle. Sometimes in winter when the trails were rough, she would slip and tumble off the horse's back into the snow. When that happened, Belle always stopped and turned her long, kind face around to see if Molly was all right. Then the mare would wait patiently while the little girl scrambled up onto her back again before she resumed her slow, measured gait along the trail.
>
> —Marilynn Reynolds

You can infer that Molly's family was poor because "there was no money for a saddle," and you can also infer that they liked music because Molly had piano lessons every week. You can conclude that Belle was a gentle horse. You would draw this conclusion when you read that Belle always stopped to make sure Molly was all right whenever Molly fell off Belle.

2.1.3.1 *Use headings, paragraphs, punctuation and quotation marks to assist with constructing and confirming meaning*

3.2.2.1 *Use text features, such as titles, pictures, heading labels, diagrams, and dictionary guide words, to access information*

USING TEXT FEATURES

Have you ever noticed that when you are reading something like the following passage, some things stand out? The title is bigger and darker, there are pictures, and some words are italicized or inside brackets. All of these can help you to find information more quickly and to better understand what you are reading.

Let's say your teacher assigned you a research project to find out how some sea creatures find their food. By reading the title and headings and looking at the pictures in this passage, you would quickly realize that this passage has information useful to you. The italicized first paragraph also stands out, and by quickly skimming it you will realize that it briefly tells you what the passage is going to be about.

What a Feeling!

All animals have a sense of touch, but many animals have developed special feelers that grow out of their bodies. These feelers come in all shapes and sizes. Sea anemones have pretty, but deadly, tentacles; luna moths have feathery antennae. Read on to learn more about these and other fantastic feelers!

Touchy Tentacles

What's this huge hairyness floating in the open ocean? Is it a creature from outer space? No, it's a lion's mane, the world's largest jellyfish. Its slithery, slimy body can be as big as a trampoline. But even at that size, there's not much to it—just a mouth and a stomach. Lion's mane jellyfish have more than 150 tentacles to "see" and capture prey.

The tentacles usually do nothing but hang in the water, waiting for supper. Each one can be as long as a telephone pole. When an unlucky fish, shrimp, or crab touches a tentacle—ZAP! Small capsules called nematocysts (nee-MAH-tuh-sists) located all over the jellyfish's tentacles shoot out tiny darts, called barbs, that hook into the prey.

The barbs contain powerful poison that paralyzes the unlucky target. Then the lion's mane slowly pulls the prey into its mouth with its long tentacles.

All jellyfish have tentacles and barbs, but none are as poisonous as the lion's mane. Sea anemones also use tentacles and barbs to feel around and capture food.

The Blue Browsers

Fish that lurk on the dark bottoms of rivers and oceans need more than eyes to find food. For this job, blue catfish have special feelers called barbels (BAR-bels). Four pairs of barbels stick out from the fish's nose, jaw, and chin. While the eyes of this scary-looking creature are watching out for enemies, its barbels sweep the river bottom, feeling for a tasty meal of fish.

Catfish aren't the only fish that use barbels to feel their way around. Ocean species, such as the hairy blenny and Atlantic cod, also have barbels. Blue goatfish have two long, ribbonlike barbels hanging down from below their jaw. When they're not using them to find food, they tuck them away back under their chin.

—Kendra Toby

2.1.2.3   *Identify the main idea or topic and supporting details in simple narrative and expository passages*

2.2.2.2   *Summarize the main idea of individual oral, print and other media texts*

2.3.2.1   *Include events, setting and characters when summarizing or retelling oral, print or other media texts*

MAIN IDEA AND SUPPORTING DETAILS

If you were asked to explain in one sentence what a reading passage was about, you would be trying to give its **main idea**. Very often, a title can give a reader the main idea, but not always. Sometimes, a title is too short to give enough information.

For example, if you were given a passage with the title "Dolphins are our Friends," the main idea might well be something like "Dolphins are our friends and it is important to protect them." If the same passage were just called "Dolphins," you would definitely have to read further to figure out what the writer's main point is about dolphins. When a passage does not have a title, thinking about the title that you would give it may help you to come up with its main idea.

Very often, the main idea of a passage is given in one sentence near the beginning or the end. In the dolphin passage we just imagined, the last sentence of the passage might be something like, "You can see how important it is to protect these wonderful creatures from fishers and from the pollution of their ocean homes." This probably sums up the whole passage.

Supporting details are sentences and phrases that give details and examples that support the main idea.

For example, in the passage "Dolphins are our Friends," supporting details might include information about how dolphins love to play and swim with people. Other supporting details could be how dolphins communicate and how people can help to protect dolphins from danger.

Summarizing the Main Idea

Summarizing a text into its main idea is to tell the main parts of the story in your own words. To help you remember the important points in a passage or text that you are reading, it is a good idea to write down, in your own words, the main ideas and supporting details. It can also be helpful to jot these details down in a diagram. Using the "Giants of the Forest" passage found below, here is one idea for putting the main idea and supporting details into a diagram (this one is called a web).

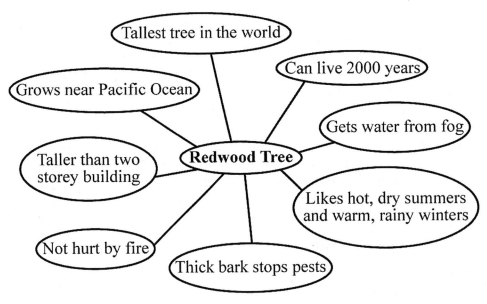

When you are asked to summarize a text, be sure to:

- Retell the text in your own words.
- Explain the main idea.
- Include the important events or supporting details.

Read the following passage from "Giants of the Forest" and think about the main ideas that would go into a summary.

> Redwoods are the tallest trees in the world. The tallest redwood is taller than a twenty-story building. It is so big around that six people holding hands could barely reach around it.
>
> How do redwoods get so big? First, they live where the weather is just right for them. Redwood trees grow near the Pacific Ocean in the states of California and Oregon. They live in an area with hot dry summer and warm rainy winters. Though they don't get much rain, fog comes in every day, and the trees get water from the fog. And redwoods are not hurt by pests. Redwoods have very thick bark, so insects can't hurt the inside of the trees.
>
> Even fire does not hurt redwood trees. Redwoods have three ways to guard against forest fires. First, their bark must get very hot in order to burn. Next, the needles and branches, which burn more easily than the bark, are far up from the ground. Fire almost never reaches them. And because redwood branches keep the sunlight from getting to the forest floor, not many plants can grow under redwoods. So fires don't start easily in the forest.
>
> It's a good thing redwoods are so healthy, for they take many years to grow ... they often live and keep growing for two thousand years! They are some of the oldest living things in the world.

Here is what a summary of the passage might look like:

The tallest trees in the world are the redwoods found in California and Oregon. The hot, dry summers and warm, wet winters are just right for them to grow so big. Their height and thick bark protect them from fire and insects, so they stay healthy and grow. Some of them live for two thousand years, which makes them some of the oldest living things on Earth.

Summarizing Fiction

The previous two examples were both samples of informational writing. Summarizing fiction is done in much the same way, as you still need to:

- Retell the text in your own words.
- Explain the main idea.
- Include the important events or supporting details.
- Describe the ending.

With fiction, however, you also need to consider setting and characters. Setting is the time and place in which a story takes place. Characters are the individuals that are in the story that you are reading.

Think about the story of Cinderella. The story takes place a long time ago mainly in Cinderella's home but also in the King's castle, and briefly on the road home from the ball. The main characters are Cinderella, her stepmother and two stepsisters, her fairy godmother, and the prince.

2.3.2.2 *Describe the main characters in terms of who they are, their actions in the story and their relations with other characters*

2.2.2.4 *Make inferences about a character's action or feelings*

LOOKING AT CHARACTERS

As you read, you should pay particular attention to the main characters and be able to describe them either using a graphic organizer or in complete sentences. One way to do this is to create a web showing the character in the middle and facts about her branching off from the centre.

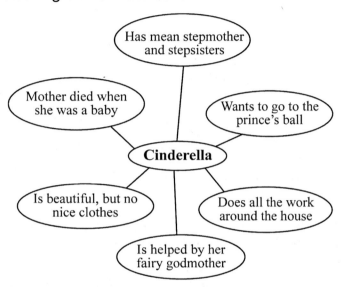

As you read, you might also see if you can infer why characters make choices and do the things they do. Sometimes you need to wear your detective hat and looks for clues as to why a character acts the way he does. Sometimes you just need to guess. Why does the fairy godmother help Cinderella? Why does Cinderella want to go to the ball? Why did the fairy godmother make Cinderella's fancy clothes change back to rags at midnight?

Even if the author does not tell you directly, can you tell how a character feels in different parts of the story? How does Cinderella feel when she first arrives at the ball? Is she excited, nervous, terrified, proud, happy, bored or tired?

As you write a story, you also need to think about these things and decide how much detail about your characters to include. Do you need to describe exactly how your characters look, what they are thinking and how they are feeling? Choosing which things are important to the story is part of your job as a writer. If you spend too much time on such details, you might not have enough time or space to actually write the action of the story.

2.1.3.6   *Monitor and confirm meaning by rereading when necessary, and by applying knowledge of pragmatic, semantic, syntactic and graphophonic cueing systems*

THE MEANING OF WORDS AND PHRASES

Sometimes you might get to the end of a passage and realize that you did not understand what you just read. Often it will help to reread the passage. You may notice information you missed the first time around.

If you are having trouble with certain words within the passage, here are some ideas for figuring out what they mean.

1. Try looking at the word in its context within the sentence or paragraph. You may be able to guess its meaning based on what the text around the word says. For example:

   The woman was always very <u>generous</u>. She gave the children toys to play with and homemade cookies to eat.

   If you do not understand the meaning of *generous* when you read that the woman gave toys and cookies to the children, you can probably guess that *generous* means almost the same as *kind* or *giving*.

2. Try using some of the language rules that you already know. For example, you have probably learned that the prefix *un* means *not*. Thus *unhappy* means *not happy*

   When Claire cannot find her favourite toy she is very <u>unhappy</u>.

3. Try looking at any illustrations that are available. Imagine a passage about the different types of whales. A sentence about the blue whale states that it is a gargantuan sea creature. If there is a picture of the various types of whales by size, you would notice that the blue whale is considerably bigger than the other whales. Thus you could make the assumption that *gargantuan* means *huge*.

DIFFERENT TEXT FORMS

2.2.1.3 *Identify types of literature, such as humour, poetry, adventure and fairy tales, and describe favourites*

2.3.1.1 *Identify distinguishing features of a variety of oral, print and other media texts*

LOOKING AT TEXT FORM

By now you have probably seen many different types of writing and each looks and feels different depending on who is expected to read it and why they would read it. When you were very young, you probably first saw picture books and someone read them to you while you mostly looked at the pictures. Picture books are an example of one type or *genre* of literature. They are very good for telling a simple story or teaching simple ideas to young children. You would easily recognize a picture book just by looking at it. They usually have bold, interesting pictures on every page and range from one or two words per page to one or two short paragraphs on a page.

Another genre you would recognize by looking at it is an instruction sheet or manual. Almost every toy, tool, appliance or piece of sports equipment you buy comes with some kind of instructions. Instructional or "how-to" writing is usually organized in similar sections: equipment or parts (including diagrams), steps to operate, build or maintain, safety notes and repair or trouble-shooting hints. If you saw a folded piece of paper with black and white printing and some diagrams tucked into the box of a new bike helmet, you would know right away that it contained some kind of instructions. This is because you have seen this *genre* of writing so many times that you recognize it both by how it looks and where you found it.

As you read more and discover different types of writing, pay attention to the clues that tell you what type of writing it is. Next time you see an unfamiliar book lying around, try this little exercise:

1. At first sight, without picking up the book, ask yourself what type of book you think it is. Possibly it is a picture book, a novel or chapter book, a textbook, a mystery, or a comic book. What clues are you using to make that prediction? Title? An author you recognize? Cover pictures? Size of book? Number of pages?

2. Next, pick up the book and look more closely at it—inside and out. Was your prediction correct, or at least partly correct? What clues inside the book help you to decide? Chapter titles? Number of pictures? Table of contents? Summary or reviews written on the jacket flaps? Specific words or section headings?

You could also do this with any other writing you see lying around—even single pieces of paper which could be letters, flyers, newsletters, signs, instructions and so on. Also try it with television and radio programs and with websites. When you flip through channels on TV, what are the clues that tell you what type of program you are watching? How quickly can you tell whether it is an advertisement, a nature documentary, a funny show, a game show or a news show? Probably you can tell in a split second! How? Stop and check inside yourself to discover what the clues were that your brain processed so quickly.

Here are a few of the common types of writing that you should be able to recognize and a description of what makes each different.

Play—a type of story meant to be acted out on a stage. Because a play is written to be performed, it uses speaking or *dialogue* and action instructions. It is easy to recognize a play by the way it looks on paper.

> [*Jenny and Jamie appear, running through the woods.*]
>
> **JENNY**: We are lost. I just know we are!
>
> **JAMIE**: Oh come on—trust me. I know where we are!
>
> **JENNY**: The last time you said that, we ended up lost for two days.

Novel—usually a long story, or perhaps you know it as a "chapter book." Most novels have several characters, settings, and events. The events in a novel may be based on real happenings, but it has made-up characters and events. Novels can be funny (humorous), describe an adventure or quest (adventure), based on historical events (history), describe a crime or mystery to be solved (mystery), or describe realistic characters and events (realistic). A passage taken from a novel can be recognized because it often has a chapter number and title. A novel is usually published as one book and has few if any pictures, compared to the amount of words. It may be bound as a hardcover or paperback book and it will usually have a bright, interesting cover that hints at what the novel is about.

Novels often read by Grade 3 students include *Charlotte's Web*, *The Tale of Despereaux*, *Charlie and the Chocolate Factory*, *The Mouse and the Motorcycle* and *Judy Moody*. More recently, graphic novels have become a popular form— telling a complex story using a comic-book style of graphics and words. Popular graphic novels include *Bone: Out from Boneville* and *Asterix the Gaul*.

Your local library probably has lists of novels by genre and grade or age level to help you branch out and try something new. For instance, the Edmonton Public Library has a section called "Lists of Great Books for Kids" that contains such lists as "If You Love Harry Potter...," "Books for Kids Who Love Cats and Dogs," "Books for Boys" and "Graphic Novels for Kids."

Short Story—a story that can usually be read in one sitting. A short story centres around one main event. There is usually one main character and sometimes a few other minor characters. Short stories are often published as a collection in a book or singly in a magazine, newspaper or textbook.
Short stories may be about modern events or they may be old traditional stories. Two types of traditional stories you should be able to recognize are fairy tales and folk tales.

Folk Tale—a narrative story that teaches a lesson to the reader or explains the world in some way. For example, in the folk tale *Little Red Riding Hood*, the main lesson taught children never to speak to strangers. These tales usually have magic in them and often have animal characters that act like humans. You may have read different versions of *The Three Little Pigs* or *Stone Soup*. *The Three Little Pigs* has animals speaking and behaving as humans, and *Stone Soup* is about a main character who used his wits to trick others to help him get food. Folk tales come from all over the world and can tell us a lot about the traditions of different cultures.

Fairy Tale—narrative story that has magical elements, usually involving fairies, elves, princesses with fairy godmothers, witches, wizards, magic potions and spells, and other such things. Fairy tales may have a lesson or moral, but often are more for entertainment than teaching. Fairy tales usually have a clear hero and/or heroine (the "good guys") and an equally clear villain (the "bad guy"). The traditional fairy tale begins with "Once upon a time" and ends with the good guys living "happily ever after," but this is not always the case. Some well-know fairy tales include *Cinderella*, *The Little Mermaid*, *Snow White and the Seven Dwarfs*, *Rapunzel*, and *Rumpelstiltskin*.

Adventure or Mystery Story—stories that have lots of exciting action and possibly many problems to solve. In a mystery story, the writer gives you clues to help you solve the mystery along with the main character. As with all stories, the mystery story must still have a beginning, middle, and ending. The beginning usually introduces the mystery to be solved. Most of the action and events happen in the middle. The story closes when the mystery has been solved. The solution is usually explained at the end. An example of a mystery you may have read is *Cam Jansen and the Mystery of the Dinosaur Bones* by David Adler.

In an adventure story, the writer often begins the story with the main character getting into trouble or experiencing what seems like a life-threatening situation. The character has to get out of trouble or get back home safely. Usually the character has many roadblocks that prevent him or her from getting out of trouble easily. Most often, the character ends up finding a unique or interesting solution to her problem. An example of an adventure story you may have read is *The Reluctant Deckhand* by Jan Padgett. The *Horrible Harry* stories by Suzy Kline and *Marvin Redpost* stories by Louis Sachar are both examples of adventure stories.

Non-Fiction Prose—a type of writing in which real things, events, and/or people are written about. How-to books, newspaper and magazine articles, history books, interviews, and biographies are some examples of non-fiction writing. A specific example would be a passage explaining about the different kinds of birds found in Canada.

Poetry—poems. Poems often have rhythm and they sometimes rhyme, especially those written for children. They often use very colourful and expressive language to explain an idea or event. Songs are examples of poetry, as are nursery rhymes, limericks, and many picture books. Poetry can often be recognized by the way it looks on the page. Writers often choose to group the text into verses or shape the printed words into interesting patterns.

a) A poem about the sun might be written with the words forming the circular shape of the sun.

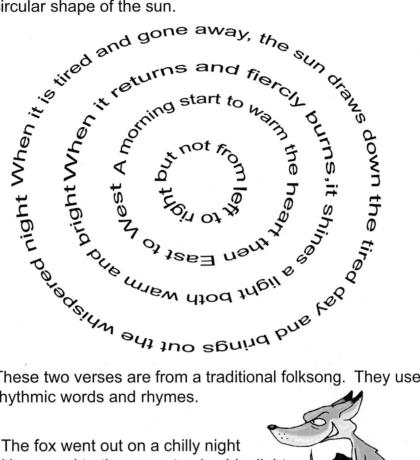

b) These two verses are from a traditional folksong. They use both rhythmic words and rhymes.

The fox went out on a chilly night
He prayed to the moon to give him light,
For he'd many a mile to go that night,
Before he reached the town-o, town-o, town-o
He'd many a mile to go that night,
Before he reached the town-o.

He ran 'til he came to the farmer's pen,
The ducks and the geese were kept therein
He said "A couple of you are going to grease my chin
Before I leave this town-o, town-o, town-o!
A couple of you are going to grease my chin,
Before I leave this town-o!"

2.1.1.2   *Identify the different ways in which oral, print and other media texts, such as stories, textbooks, letters, pictionaries and junior dictionaries, are organized*

ORGANIZATION OF TEXTS

The way that events, instructions, descriptions and other information are organized helps you to understand the writing, enjoy the story, and to find things more easily. Different types or *genres* of writing each have their own characteristic organization.

Dictionaries, **pictionaries** and **encyclopaedia** are all organized alphabetically to make it easy to find the information you need. For example, if you want to know the meaning of the word *marine*, you would look in the 'M' section of the dictionary in between the words *marina* and *mariner*. All dictionaries are arranged this way, so you always know how to find a word's meaning. A dictionary is not organized in a way to make it exciting to read from cover to cover, but rather to make it easy to find information.

Textbooks are usually organized by subject. Each chapter is often about a different subject within the larger subject of the book. For example, a Grade 3 science textbook may have chapters about Rocks and Minerals, Hearing and Sound, Animal Life Cycles, and so on. It would have a table of contents at the front and an index at the back that would help you to find information quickly, but a textbook is most often read one section at a time to go along with the teaching in class. If this information were organized alphabetically, it 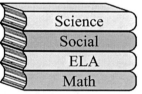 would be very confusing to read for the student. It is easier if all the information on one subject is grouped together.

Letters are organized to make it easy for the reader to understand who the letter is for and from, what it is about, when it was written and where responses can be sent. Business letters often go to very busy people who have to read a lot of letters every day. They are organized to make it very quick for the recipient (the person who receives the letter) to understand why the writer has sent the letter, what he wants and what the recipient can do about it.

Newspaper articles and news stories usually start with a headline that grabs the reader's attention and makes him want to find out what the headline really means. The article itself is quite short and needs to get all its facts across quickly. Sometimes the headline of a story is more exciting than the story itself!

Local Boy Discovers Treasure Under His Own Doorstep!

8-year-old Daniel Ferguson is being called a hero for recovering Treasure from the crawl space under his front porch.

Treasure, a golden striped kitten belonging to Mrs. Edith Epstein, had been missing for two days. Daniel, a grade 3 student at Preston Elementary School, had been playing catch with a friend when his ball rolled under the steps. As he peered into the dark space below the large front porch to find the ball, he heard a faint mewing. The brave youngster overcame his fear of the dark and squeezed his way under the porch to rescue the poor little mite who had fallen into a hole too deep for it to climb out. Daniel suffered numerous scratches in the rescue, but he says that it was all worth it to see Mrs. Epstein back with her Treasure. Treasure has taken such a liking to her rescuer that she visits Daniel daily for a saucer of milk on his porch.

Stories and articles are arranged in different ways, often to encourage the reader to keep reading. The following are just a few ways that writers organize their work.

Writers often use **cause and effect** to develop stories. In this type of text, you learn why events happened and why things are as they are. Cause and effect is often used in writing that informs, explains, or persuades. The words *if* and *then* are often used to show how one thing can lead to another. For instance, "If you stay up late, then you will probably be tired tomorrow." Some other cause and effect words are *because*, *as a result*, *why*, *when*, *therefore*, *so*, and *for this reason*.

It was sports day at school and the children were looking forward to a day of playing games outside. However, at 11:30 am, a thunderstorm with lightning, strong winds, and heavy rains began, and all the children had to go indoors. Because the afternoon activities were cancelled, the children had to stay in their classrooms.

Cause		Effect
thunderstorm	⟶	children go inside
activities cancelled	⟶	children stay in classrooms

Chronology is used in texts to give the order in time in which things happen. Time order makes sure that events occur in sequential order. Some words that help explain time order are *first, second, now, then, after, before,* and *later.*

"Breakfast"
from **Chapter 1 of** *Nim's Island*

"And what we need first," said Nim, "is breakfast!" So she threw four ripe coconuts thump! into the sand and climbed down after them.

Then she whistled her shell, two long, shrill notes that carried far out to the reef, where the sea lions were fishing. Selkie popped her head above the water. She had a fish in her mouth, but she swallowed it fast and dived toward the beach.

And from a rock by the hut, Fred came scuttling. Fred was an iguana, spiky as a dragon, with a cheerful snub nose. He twined round Nim's feet in a prickly hug.

"Are you saying good morning," Nim demanded, "or just begging for breakfast?"

Fred stared at the coconuts. He was a very honest iguana.

Coconuts are tricky to open, but Nim was an expert. With a rock and a spike, she punched a hole and drank the juice, cracked the shell and pried out the flesh. Fred snatched his piece and gulped it down.

—*by* Wendy Orr

From reading this passage, you can see that there is a definite order in which the events occur, and that one event is related to, or leads to, the next:

First: Nim throws four coconuts in the sand

Then: She whistles her shell

Then: Selkie pops up her head

Then: Selkie comes to the beach

Then: Fred comes to Nim

Then: Nim punches a hole in the coconut

Then: Nim opens the coconut

Last: Fred eats his piece of coconut

2.3.2.3 *Identify ways that messages are enhanced in oral, print and other media texts by the use of specific techniques*

2.2.3.2 *Identify how authors use comparisons, and explain how they create mental images*

2.3.3.1 *Recognize examples of repeated humour, sound and poetic effects that contribute to audience enjoyment*

2.3.1.2 *Discuss ways that visual images convey meaning in print and other media texts*

DIFFERENT WAYS TO PRESENT IDEAS

Today there are many, many different ways to communicate stories and ideas. Writers need to choose which will be the most effective way to reach their audiences. Think about all the ways you communicate with your friends, family, teachers and others. Do you use exactly the same words when you are speaking on the phone as when you are writing a report or you are talking to your friend on the way to school? You probably do not. When you talk to your friend on the way to school, you can use gestures and other body language to help get your message across, so you might use fewer words, incomplete sentences or a lot of slang. You probably would not use the same words when writing a thank you card to your grandmother. You would think a little more carefully about exactly what you want to say because only your words are giving the message. It is the same for all writers. Let's say that several writers are trying to teach students about pioneer life on the prairies in the late 19th century. See if you can imagine how the following different texts could teach this.

1. A true short story about a child waiting for the first signs of spring in a snow-buried sod hut.
2. An adventure novel about a family crossing the prairies to start their new homestead in Alberta.
3. A funny story about the tricks a young pioneer boy used to play on the girls in school.
4. A website about the different ways prairie pioneers built their homes.
5. A television show about where the prairie pioneers came from and how they had to change their traditions to fit their new homeland.
6. A picture book about a child learning to decorate Ukrainian Easter eggs (pysanka) on a pioneer farm.

Think about which would have the most detail; which would most likely include pictures; which would have the most facts; which would be designed to be entertaining as well as teaching the reader something; and which would be best for younger students and which would be better for older students.

Often writers **compare** one thing to another to help the reader get a clear picture of the thing he is describing. For example, compare the following sentences. Which of them gives you the clearest understanding of a giant's voice?

He spoke in a slow, deep voice.
His voice was as slow and deep as the rumble of distant thunder.

The writer assumes that you have heard distant thunder before and can create a clear idea in your mind of how it sounds. She hopes that **comparing** the giant's voice to the sound of thunder will make it easier for you, the reader, to guess what the voice is like.

Writers often want to create a clear image in the reader's mind of the things they describe. Sometimes, they want the reader to create his own picture or at least part of the picture. If an author is writing about facts or explaining how to do something, she will want to describe things as clearly and in as much detail as possible to make sure the reader gets the facts right. In these cases, a writer will often add pictures or diagrams to help make the facts clear. If an author is writing an exciting adventure story, she may use more of her words to describe how a character is feeling than in describing exactly what he looks like or what the weather is like. She will choose to describe more fully the things that will help the story to be more exciting. The reader then may need to fill in his own details to visualize the character or the setting. Sometimes a mental picture becomes clearer as the story progresses and writer gradually adds more detail.

Writers love to play with words. One way writers do this, especially in poetry and funny (humorous) stories, is to use repeated words and the sounds of words to make their writing fun to read or perform. Perhaps you know some of the stories of Canadian author Robert Munsch. Stories such as *Mortimer, Pigs!, Moira's Birthday*, and *I have to go!* all have phrases that are repeated over and over, making them particularly fun to read aloud and for children to listen to. Robert Munsch is an oral storyteller, first and foremost. This means that he makes up his stories and tells them out loud many times before he ever writes them down. Because of this, he is very good at writing in a way that sounds good read aloud. By the middle of one of his stories, the listeners can very often join in with the repeated parts.

In *Mortimer*, the following refrains are repeated so often that most young children can't help but join in after the second repetition or so.

"Mortimer, be quiet!"

and

"Clang, clang, rattle-bing-bang,
Gonna make my noise all day,
Clang, clang, rattle-bing-bang,
Gonna make my noise all day."

In *Moira's Birthday*, the phrase "...grade one, grade two, grade three, grade four, grade five, grade six, aaaaaand kindergarten" is repeated in every stage of the story.

See if you can find other stories and poems that use repetition to give them rhythm or make them fun to read.

Here is a poem by Canadian poet Dennis Lee that uses repetition, rhythm and a simple rhyming pattern to make it fun to both say and listen to.

Alligator pie, alligator pie,
If I don't get some I think I'm going to die.
Give away the green grass, give away the sky,
But don't give away my alligator pie.

Alligator soup, alligator soup,
If I don't get some I think I'm going to droop.
Give away my hockey stick, give away my hoop,
But don't give away my alligator soup.

See if you can make up another verse that follows Dennis Lee's repeated pattern. How about one for alligator cake, or alligator bread, alligator tea, or alligator stew?

UNDERSTANDING WORDS

2.1.2.1   *Use grammatical knowledge to predict words and sentence structures when reading narrative and expository materials*

2.1.2.4   *Extend sight vocabulary to include predictable phrases and words related to language use*

PREDICTING MEANING OF WORDS AND PHRASES

There is no magic list of words you can memorize to make sure you understand the words you read in passages. There are books and websites that list words that kids should know how to read and write by each grade, but the best thing you can do is read and get into the habit of looking up words in the dictionary.

Get yourself a dictionary small enough to carry around, but big enough to be useful. Every time you come across a word whose meaning you are not really sure about, go through the following steps:

1. **Read** the word **in context**—in its sentence or the nearest couple of sentences.
2. Make a guess as to the **word's meaning**, even if it is only a rough guess.
3. **Look at the word alone**. Pay attention to any prefixes or suffixes that might give you hints. Does the word look like any other words you know?
4. **Update your guess**, if necessary, based on step 3.
5. Now, and *not until now*, **look the word up** in the dictionary.
6. **Go back and read the word in context again**. Does the dictionary definition make sense to you? If not, ask your teacher or parent, or the person with the best vocabulary you can find, to help you.
7. If all else fails, **do not panic**! You should not be able to understand every single word you might come across in Grade 3, especially if you read things written for older kids and adults. Just file that word away in your brain to look at again later!

If you are not looking up at least a couple of words a day, you are probably missing chances to improve your reading understanding. Ask your parents to do the same thing with their reading. It is something many adults forget to do.

A skill of being a good reader is being able to predict what comes next. We discussed making predictions earlier when we looked at "Why We Read." That section gave you hints to help you figure out the meaning of a passage.

We can also use predicting skills to figure out individual words or phrases. We normally do this without thinking about it when we read, but practicing this skill will make you a better reader.

Try this activity with your friends. Find a book you are all interested in reading. One person starts reading and then stops at different points to ask, "What comes next?" It is more interesting if you have more than one person answering. Will your answers be the same or will you all come up with something different?

Sometimes the answer is very obvious. If the sentence is, "As Emily was running quickly along the path, she tripped on a root and _____." The most logical answer is "fell" because we all associate "falling" with "tripping."

 If a book starts out with "Once upon a time" you will likely guess that the next words will be "in a land far, far away…" This is because "Once upon a time" is the standard way for a fairy tale to begin and most of us are familiar with the wording.

Now move on to sentences that aren't so obvious. "Gathering together the necessary materials, Nathan built a fabulous _____." You will likely get many different guesses here because of the lack of information. Birdhouse? Rocket? Soapbox racer? Read the next sentence, "He was desperate to be the winner of the $50 prize for highest launch." Now your friends will likely guess rocket, as they will associate "rocket" with "launch." You can see how important context (the text around what you are reading) is to predicting words and phrases.

Whether you do this activity alone or with friends, it will strengthen your predicting skills and improve your reading ability. And the better you are at reading, the more you will enjoy it.

2.1.4.1 *Apply phonic rules and generalizations competently and confidently to read unfamiliar words in context*

2.1.4.3 *Associate sounds with an increasing number of vowel combinations, consonant blends and digraphs, and letter clusters to read unfamiliar words in context*

UNFAMILIAR WORDS

When you are reading unfamiliar words your teacher may suggest that you sound them out. Often letters combine in patterns that you will learn to recognize and that will help you figure out words you do not know.

VOWEL COMBINATIONS

Often several different groups of vowels make the same sound. The more you read, the easier it will be to recognize these vowel patterns. The following charts contain the most common vowel combinations.

Long ā sound can be made by	"ay" as in say
	"ai" as in paid
	"a" as in rate
	"ei" as in weight
	"ea" as in great

Long ē sound can be made by	"ee" as in street or green
	"ea" as in treat or reach
	"ei" as in receive or weird
	"ie" as in piece or thief

The letters "oi" and "oy," "ou" and "ow," "oo" and "ew" have similar sounds, but are written in different ways. This makes remembering how to spell them difficult. Here is a hint to help you spell words with these similar sounds. Usually, the vowel combinations "oi," "ou," and "oo" are found in the middle of a word, while "oy," "ow," and "ew" are found at the end of a word.

oi	oy	ou	ow	oo	ew
noise	boy	hour	allow	tool	blew
boil	ploy	cloud	plow	hooves	few

CONSONANT BLENDS

A consonant blend is when two or more consonants combine to make part of a word. Examples of consonant blends are:

bl—black, blush

ch—chat, cheek

dr—drag, drop

sm—small, smog

spl—spleen, splat

DIGRAPHS

Digraph is just a fancy word for two letters together that make a single sound. Digraphs include both consonants and vowels. Examples are:

ai—sail

ea—beat

ph—pheasant

th—these

wh—white

2.1.4.2 *Apply word analysis strategies to segment words into parts or syllables, when reading unfamiliar words in context*

DIVIDING WORDS INTO SYLLABLES

Words are made up of smaller parts called syllables. Each syllable contains one vowel sound. Because of this, it is easiest to count syllables by saying the word out loud. Dividing a word into syllables can

- help you spell it correctly
- help you say it correctly
- help you figure out its meaning

Here are some simple rules for dividing words into syllables.

1. Count the number of vowel sounds in words.

triangle   contains three vowels and each has its own vowel sound so the word has three syllables: tri / ang / le

careful   contains three vowels, but one is silent so the word only has two syllables: care / ful

goat   contains two vowels but only one vowel sound—a long ō—so the word contains one syllable

goatee   contains four vowels but only two vowel sounds—a long ō and a long ē—so the word contains two syllables: goat / ee

2. Divide words before a suffix and after a prefix.

suffix: still / ness
          play / ing

prefix: pre / pare
          re / turn

3. Divide compound words between the joined words.
play / ground
pin / wheel
fire / truck

4. Divide words between double consonants.

put / ting
hap / pen

Exception: When double consonants are part of the root word, do not divide between them.

tall / est
dress / ing

5. Divide words between two vowels or two consonants when they are pronounced separately.

re / act   bur / ger
li / on   mon /key

2.1.5.1 *Put words in alphabetical order by first and second letter*

PUTTING WORDS INTO ALPHABETICAL ORDER

Alphabetical order involves arranging words in order according to the alphabet. The first letter of a word is the starting point. If you have words that start with the same letter, arrange them next by the second letter and then the third and so on. For example, in the following list you would first arrange the words by their first letters.

agree   admit   blue   brain   bark

Looking at the two "a" words, examine their second letters. You will see that *d* comes before *g* in the alphabet, thus *admit* must come before *agree*. Doing the same with the "b" words means they need to be rearranged their second letters, with *a* coming first, followed by *l* and then *r*.

Thus proper alphabetical order of these words would be

admit   agree   bark   blue   brain

Examples of places that you will find words in alphabetical order are a dictionary, thesaurus, telephone book, glossary, and index.

PRACTICE QUESTIONS—READING

Read the following passage to answer questions 1 to 10.

THE GHOSTLY SNEEZE
A FOLKTALE FROM PICARDY IN FRANCE

It was once believed that the road to Englebelmer was haunted.
Travelers along the road would suddenly be startled by a violent
sneezing sound.

"Achoo! Achoo! Achoo!"

5 The traveller would stop … stare around … call out … "Who's there?"

But no one ever answered.

The traveller would start on down the road again.

But soon …

"Achoo! Achoo! Achoo!"

10 Word got around that a sneezing ghost haunted the road.
The ghost seemed to be teasing people,
following them along their way,
sneezing at them every time they began to feel they were safe again.

The people of the region eventually got used to the sneezing ghost.
15 Whenever he would start up with his *Achoo!* business,
they would just cross themselves and go on.

But one night a farmer was returning late from market
When the ghost started following him.

"Achoo! Achoo! Achoo!"

20 This went on for half an hour without letting up.
Finally the farmer could stand no more of it.

"Enough with your sneezing!" he shouted.
"May God bless you and your cold!"

Instantly the sneezing stopped
25 and a ghostly form appeared before him.

"Thank you, my friend," spoke the ghost.
"You have delivered me from this unending sneezing.
I was condemned to wander this road, sneezing, until some kind
soul should say to me, "'God bless you.'"

30 With that the ghost disappeared.
And if a sneeze was ever heard on that road again,
it was the sneeze of a human … not a ghost.

Next morning the farmer hurried to tell everyone in the village about
this good news.

35 And from then on, whenever anyone sneezed …
everyone would shout,
"God bless you!"
And today …we still do!

Aaaaachoo!

40 "God bless you!"

—*By* Margaret Read MacDonald

1. People thought that the road to Englebelmer was haunted because they

    A. saw strange shapes

    B. saw ghosts sneezing

    C. heard ghosts talking

    D. heard strange sneezing

2. This story is an example of a

    A. fable

    B. folktale

    C. fairy tale

    D. horror story

3. In the sentence "Travellers along the road would suddenly be startled by a violent sneezing sound," the word *startled* means

    A. woken up

    B. surprised

    C. bothered

    D. amused

4. In the sentence "Travellers along the road would suddenly be startled by a violent sneezing sound," the word *violent* means

    A. angry

    B. forceful

    C. harmful

    D. terrifying

5. According to the story, the local people "got used to the sneezing ghost," which means that they

   A. were no longer alarmed because the ghost never did more than sneeze

   B. got angry with the ghost for teasing them

   C. stopped believing there was a ghost

   D. got tired of hearing the sneezing

6. The main point of this story is to

   A. explain why people say "bless you" when someone sneezes

   B. explain why people should say kind things to ghosts

   C. teach people that sneezing chases away ghosts

   D. teach people that not all ghosts are bad

7. The ghost finally appeared visible when

   A. people crossed themselves

   B. the farmer said, "God bless you"

   C. people called out, "Who's there?"

   D. the farmer shouted, "Enough with your sneezing!"

8. In the sentence "You have delivered me from this unending sneezing," the word *delivered* is a synonym for

   A. sent

   B. freed

   C. brought

   D. captured

9. In the phrase "Instantly the sneezing stopped," the word *instantly* is an antonym for

A. quickly

B. suddenly

C. eventually

D. immediately

10. In the phrase "I was condemned to wander this road, sneezing," the word *condemned* is a synonym for

A. created

B. captured

C. sentenced

D. challenged

Read the following passage to answer questions 11 to 30.

THE NEW BOY
from **THE INVISIBLE ENEMY**

The desks in our classroom are arranged in a sort of circle, so we all face each other. Mr. Donaldson had squeezed in an extra desk with the name Jean-Pierre printed on a card to match the others. I watched, steaming, while Alyssa guided the poor boy to his

5 place as if he were blind.

"I speak English," I heard him say. "And I can see."

His voice was a bit husky, which made his accent sound like someone in a movie. He was even cuter close up, with hazely eyes and long lashes. Alyssa just kept standing there, staring at

10 him. Her pal Megan leaned over and poked her to stop making a fool of herself.

"Take your seats, people. Settle down. Welcome back, everyone. I'd like to officially welcome our newcomer, Jean-Pierre de LaTour."

15 Jean-Pierre saluted and smiled a crooked smile. His desk was directly opposite mine, so I caught the main shine. Hubert is next to me, and Alyssa is three over, well out of smile range.

"You'll have plenty of time during the day to show Jean-Pierre how friendly New Yorkers can be." Mr. Donaldson looked around.
20 "Ah, Hubert? Would you be Jean-Pierre's buddy for today?"

Hubert blushed and nodded at Jean-Pierre to introduce himself. In our class, it is well known that Hubert does not like to speak out loud. Especially not to strangers. Mr. D picked him on purpose—an exercise in torture disguised as
25 social encouragement.

"Show him around, make sure he finds the cafeteria and other essential facilities …." Mr. Donaldson always calls the bathroom "the facilities."

Jean-Pierre nodded back at Hubert and spun his yo-yo like a
30 top across his desk.

"Toys are not allowed in the classroom," said Mr. Donaldson, with a laser-beam squint. "Since it's your first day, I'll let you off with a warning." He laughed to try to show he was a nice guy, but we all knew he was dying to add that yo-yo to the collection of
35 our treasures in his bottom drawer.

"All right then, listen up, people. We have a busy quarter ahead of us, with the first focus on your projects about medieval life. We have a couple of field trips coming up, starting this week—"

40   "Are we going on a school bus or the subway?" asked Josh

"—with an excursion, on a school bus, to the Cloisters. That's Friday, leaving first thing. We'll be seeing a marvelous reconstruction of medieval architecture as well as—yes Josh?"

"Do we have to bring a lunch?"

45   "You'll need to bring a bag lunch, no glass bottles, no candy—yes, Josh?"

"Can we have soda, sir?"

"Yes, you may have soda. Eyes on me, people. This trip will be very instructive for all who—"

50   I noticed Hubert was watching Jean-Pierre instead of the teacher. I guess we all were.

I wrote a note and passed it along with my elbow.

Don't worry. I'll help you with the new kid.

Hubert and I waited after class while Jean-Pierre collected
55 a stack of textbooks from Mr. D. and stuffed them into a plastic shopping bag. Alyssa hovered at the door, trying, as usual, to barge in where she's not wanted.

Jean-Pierre saw us looking at the plastic bag.

"I was waiting to see what the other kids use," he said shrugging.
60 "I want to look like a New Yorker!"

"We all have backpacks." I turned around to show him.

"Billie would probably die without her backpack." Alyssa giggled, tugging on my strap.

I yanked away from her.

65   "See? Taking Billie's backpack would be like ripping a shell off a turtle."

Alyssa has been suspicious of my backpack ever since the day last fall when my puppy, Harry, came to school inside it.
Thanks to my secret weapon, he was invisible at the time, but he
70 wiggled enough to nearly give himself away. Now Alyssa pokes my pack whenever she can, just in case it will move. She won't give up the hope that she might uncover something to get me in trouble.

What if she knew the truth? I have to keep it hidden from my ever-curious little sister, so I carry it with me at all times.
75 In my backpack is enough Vanishing Powder to make Alyssa disappear from my life.

—*by* Marthe Jocelyn

11. The name Jean-Pierre de LaTour is probably

   A. French

   B. English

   C. Russian

   D. German

12. Mr. Donaldson placed a card printed with Jean-Pierre's name on a desk because he

   A. knew the new student could read

   B. wanted the new student to know where to sit

   C. wanted the new student to choose where to sit

   D. was practising writing the new student's name

13. Jean-Pierre told Alyssa that he could see because

   A. she was treating him like he was blind

   B. he did not want her to be confused

   C. she thought he could not read

   D. he was new to the school

14. The sentence "And I can see" (line 6) is in quotation marks because someone is

   A. angry

   B. walking

   C. speaking

   D. confused

15. Alyssa most likely thought Jean-Pierre was

   A. handsome

   B. confused

   C. scary

   D. ugly

16. When they are listed in alphabetical order, the words sound, settle, staring, and squeezed are

 A. settle, staring, sound, squeezed

 B. staring, sound, squeezed, settle

 C. squeezed, staring, settle, sound

 D. settle, sound, squeezed, staring

17. A synonym for the word "pokes" as it is used in the phrase "Alyssa pokes my pack whenever she can," (line 59) is

 A. whispers

 B. bounces

 C. tickles

 D. jabs

18. When Mr. Donaldson asked Hubert to be Jean-Pierre's buddy for the day, Hubert probably felt

 A. embarrassed

 B. confused

 C. proud

 D. angry

19. A yo-yo is a toy made up of

 A. a large plastic ball

 B. a rubber tube and three marbles

 C. three wooden sticks tied together with elastics

 D. two disks connected in the center by a pin with a string attached

20. The place that Mr. Donaldson calls "the facilities" is the

    A. principal's office

    B. playground

    C. classroom

    D. bathroom

21. The reason that there is an exclamation mark at the end of the sentence "I want to look like a New Yorker!" is that Jean-Pierre is

    A. making a statement

    B. asking a question

    C. excited

    D. angry

22. The phrase " 'Taking Billie's backpack would be like ripping a shell off a turtle' " is an example of

    A. alliteration

    B. repetition

    C. imagery

    D. simile

23. Billie most likely thinks that Alyssa is

    A. clumsy

    B. annoying

    C. dishonest

    D. organized

24. The student who asks Mr. Donaldson a lot of questions is

    A. Josh

    B. Alyssa

    C. Hubert

    D. Jean-Pierre

25. How many syllables are in the word "especially?"

    A. Two

    B. Three

    C. Four

    D. Five

26. In the phrase " 'with an excursion, on a school bus,' " (line 41) the word "excursion" means

    A. a test

    B. an outing

    C. a vacation

    D. a museum

27. In the phrase " 'a marvelous reconstruction of medieval architecture,' " (lines 42–43) the word "reconstruction" refers to

    A. something rebuilt or repaired

    B. a house or apartment

    C. an excavation

    D. an expedition

28. Which of the following lists gives events from the story in the order in which they occurred?

A. Alyssa tugged at Billie's backpack; Jean-Pierre saluted and smiled at the class; Hubert blushed; Megan poked Alyssa.

B. Jean-Pierre saluted and smiled at the class; Megan poked Alyssa; Alyssa tugged at Billie's backpack; Hubert blushed.

C. Hubert blushed; Alyssa tugged at Billie's backpack; Megan poked Alyssa; Jean-Pierre saluted and smiled at the class.

D. Megan poked Alyssa; Jean-Pierre saluted and smiled at the class; Hubert blushed; Alyssa tugged at Billie's backpack.

29. Which of the following characters waits for Jean Pierre after class?

A. Josh

B. Megan

C. Hubert

D. Mr. Donaldson

30. For most kids, being the new student at school is probably

A. easy

B. scary

C. tiring

D. boring

Read the following passage to answer questions 31 to 40.

THE SLEEPING SPELLER

"Hey, look at this," said Judy. "This book can help us with our spelling test. For real."

"No way."

"Way! See this guy?"

5   "The bald guy with the bow tie?"

"Yep. It says that he lived right here in Virginia. They called him the Sleeping Prophet. When he was our age, like a hundred years ago, he got into trouble in school for being a bad speller. One night he fell asleep with his spelling book under his head.
10   When he woke up, he knew every word in the book. RARE!"

"I'm still going to study," said Frank.

"Not me!" said Judy, wiggling into her coat.

"What are you going to do?" asked Frank.

"I'm going to go home and sleep," said Judy.

♦ ♦ ♦

15   When Judy got home, Stink was at the door.

"I don't have to study for my spelling test," she said, and gave him a big fat hug.

"What's that for?" asked Stink.

"That's for just because."

20   "Just because why?"

"Just because tomorrow I am going to know tons and tons of words, like *woodbine*."

"Wood what?"

"It's a creepy vine. It wraps around trees."

25   "So go find a tree to hug," said Stink.

Instead, Judy went to find the dictionary. The fattest dictionary in the Moody house. She took it from her mom's office and lugged it up to her room. She did not open it up. She did not look inside. She put the big red dictionary under her pillow.

30　Then she got into her cozy bowling-ball pajamas. She pretended the bowling balls were crystal balls. When she brushed her teeth, she thought she saw a letter in her toothpaste spit. *D* for *Dictionary*.

Judy climbed under the covers and leaned back on her
35　pillow. At last, she was ready to dream.

Even before she fell asleep, she dreamed of being Queen of the Spelling Bee, just like Jessica Finch was one time for the whole state of Virginia. She dreamed of Mr. Todd's smiling face when he passed back the tests. Most of all, she dreamed of getting 110%—
40　zero-wrong-plus-extra-credit—on her spelling test.

She could hardly wait for school tomorrow. For once, she, Judy Moody, not Jessica (Flunk) Finch, would get a Thomas Jefferson tricorn-hat sticker for *Great Job, Good Thinking*.

—*by* Megan McDonald

31. The word "prophet" (line 7) describes a person who

    A. is bald

    B. cheats on tests

    C. is a good speller

    D. predicts the future

32. Stink is most likely Judy's

    A. dog

    B. father

    C. friend

    D. brother

33. The item that Judy Moody puts under her pillow to help her learn her spelling words is

    A. a spelling book

    B. her spelling list

    C. a school dictionary

    D. her mom's dictionary

34. On her spelling test, Judy hopes to score a

    A. perfect grade

    B. good grade with extra credits

    C. passing grade with zero wrong

    D. perfect grade plus bonus points

35. As a reward for doing a good job, Mr. Todd gives the students

    A. bonus points

    B. tricorn-hat stickers

    C. "Good job" pencils

    D. "Spelling Bee Champ" certificates

36. As Judy falls asleep, she is feeling

    A. frustrated

    B. distracted

    C. confident

    D. nervous

37. Judy "lugged" (line 29) the dictionary up to her room because it was very

    A. precious

    B. slippery

    C. delicate

    D. heavy

38. Based on Judy's behavior in this passage, she is probably

    A. not a very good speller

    B. the best speller in her class

    C. used to scoring 110% on spelling tests

    D. preparing to write a spelling test for the first time

39. In this passage, when Judy thinks something is interesting or exciting, she calls it

    A. rare

    B. way

    C. creepy

    D. dreamy

40. The pictures on Judy's pajamas are of

    A. tricorn hats

    B. crystal balls

    C. spelling bees

    D. bowling balls

Read the following passage to answer questions 41 to 54.

NEVER TRUST DRAGONS

'I see you've arrived,' the dragon said,
bright eyes like beacons set in his head.

'Yes,' said the vet. 'Left as soon as I knew.
Now tell me the problem, a touch of the 'flu?'

5   'My flame has gone out, I can't raise a spark,
not much use when you hunt in the dark.'

The vet peered down the gigantic throat,
black as a chimney and reeking of soot.

He threw in some petrol, a match to ignite,
10 Firelighters, coal, and some dynamite.

The dragon covered a burp with his paw,
a flicker of flame flashed down his jaw.

He licked his lips with a golden tongue:
'Take your fee, vet, you'd better run.

15 I can feel my fires boil, they are returning.
In a couple of minutes you could be burning.'

Clutching a diamond the size of a star,
the vet scampered away to his car.

As he drove off the dragon's bright fires
20 gushed out of the cave and scorched his tyres.

The vet snapped his fingers, laughed at the brute
because he was wearing his flame-proof suit.

—*by* David Harmer

41. Which of the following titles would also be a good title for this poem?

   A. Dragons are Big!

   B. The Dragon's Cave

   C. The Boring Dragon

   D. Watch Out for That Dragon!

42. Which of the following quotations contains an example of a simile?

   A. "My flame has gone out, I can't raise a spark" (line 5)

   B. "the gigantic throat, black as a chimney and reeking of soot" (lines 7-8)

   C. "He threw in some petrol, a match to ignite" (line 9)

   D. "a match to ignite, firelighters, coal and some dynamite" (lines 9-10)

43. The phrase "flicker of flame flashed" contains an example of

   A. simile

   B. allegory

   C. repetition

   D. alliteration

44. A synonym for the word "gushed" is

   A. poured

   B. crawled

   C. drizzled

   D. blossomed

45. What did the dragon pay the vet with?

   A. A flame-proof suit

   B. Fires that scorched his tires

   C. A diamond the size of a star

   D. A golden tongue and boiling fires

46. How many syllables does the word "gigantic" have?

    A. Two

    B. Three

    C. Four

    D. Five

47. The author most likely wrote this poem to

    A. entertain readers with a silly dragon tale

    B. describe what a dragon's throat looks like

    C. teach readers how to restart a dragon's flame

    D. show that even large animals like dragons get sick

48. Which of the following group of words is given in alphabetical order?

    A. Dragon, down, dynamite, dark

    B. Down, dark, dynamite, dragon

    C. Dynamite, dragon, dark, down

    D. Dark, down, dragon, dynamite

49. At what time of day does the dragon in the poem usually go hunting?

    A. Morning

    B. Afternoon

    C. Dawn

    D. Night

50. The reason that the vet laughed at the dragon was that the vet

    A. stole the dragon's car

    B. fixed the dragon's flame

    C. was wearing a flame-proof suit

    D. was playing a game with the dragon

51. The poem says that the vet "threw in some petrol." The word "petrol" means

   A. soap

   B. paint

   C. vinegar

   D. gasoline

52. The line "'I see you've arrived'" is in quotation marks because the

   A. dragon saw the vet

   B. vet came into the room

   C. the dragon was talking

   D. vet was helping the dragon

53. The reason that the dragon wanted the vet to come and see him was that the

   A. dragon was sick

   B. dragon's flame was out

   C. dragon lived with the vet

   D. dragon and the vet were friends

54. The vet mostly likely thinks that the dragon's behaviour is

   A. dull

   B. friendly

   C. pleasant

   D. unreliable

ANSWERS AND SOLUTIONS—PRACTICE QUESTIONS

1. D	13. A	25. C	37. D	49. D
2. B	14. C	26. B	38. A	50. C
3. B	15. A	27. A	39. A	51. D
4. B	16. D	28. D	40. D	52. C
5. A	17. D	29. C	41. D	53. B
6. A	18. A	30. B	42. B	54. D
7. B	19. D	31. D	43. D	
8. B	20. D	32. D	44. A	
9. C	21. C	33. D	45. C	
10. C	22. D	34. D	46. B	
11. A	23. B	35. B	47. A	
12. B	24. A	36. C	48. D	

1. D

The solution is found in the first half of the passage.
People travelling on the road to Englehelmer heard sneezing but could see where the sneezing was coming from and received no reply when they called out in the darkness.

2. B

The story meets the criteria for a folktale—explains a phenomenon. The presence of a ghost may lead some readers to think that this is a horror story, but clearly the story is not meant to frighten readers.

3. B

The word *startled* means surprised or scared. The adverb "suddenly" before this adds to the feeling of surprise.

4. B

The word *violent* can be used to mean various things: forceful, intense, extreme, resulting from fighting, and so on.
Many readers will be most familiar with its use in the context of violence causing harm.
In this passage, the word is used to mean strong or forceful.
The noise was startling, but there is no sense that the sneeze was made in anger or in a scary way.

5. A

"Getting used to" an idea means that it is no longer a cause for surprise or worry. In paragraph 7 on page 1, the author explains that the people would just cross themselves and go on.
This indicates that the people were not sure that the ghost was a good thing, but they were not going to let it stop their travels.

6. A

The solution is found at the end of this passage on page 2. This story is a folktale that explains why people say "bless you" when someone sneezes. Folktales often have a lesson in them to explain traditions or natural phenomena.

7. B

The ghost appeared just once after the farmer said, "May God bless you and your cold!"
The ghost explained that he had been waiting for someone to say this to set him free from sneezing and having to haunt the road.

8. B

A synonym is a word that means the same thing as another word. In this case, the word *delivered* means the same thing as freed. Captured (choice D) would be its antonym, which means the opposite.   Brought (choice C) can be another synonym for *delivered*, but it would not make sense in this sentence.

9. C

An antonym is a word that means the opposite of another word. In this case, *instantly* means immediately, at once, or right away. The opposite, or antonym, of *instantly* is eventually.

10. C

A synonym is a word that means the same thing as another word. In this case, the word *condemned* means the same thing as punished or sentenced.

11. A

The name Jean-Pierre de LaTour is French.

12. B

Mr. Donaldson placed a card printed with Jean-Pierre's name on a desk so that Jean-Pierre would know where to sit.

13. A

Jean-Pierre told Alyssa that he could see because she was guiding him to his desk "as if he were blind."

14. C

Quotation marks are punctuation marks used to set off speech or quotations.

15. A

Alyssa most likely thought Jean-Pierre was handsome. Jean-Pierre is described as cute, and when she first saw him, Alyssa "kept standing there, staring at him."

16. D

Listed in alphabetical order, the words are settle, sound, squeezed, and staring.

17. D

To poke means to prod, push, or jab. A synonym for the word "pokes" is *jabs*.

18. A

It is stated in the passage that "it is well known that Hubert does not like to speak out loud. Especially not to strangers." Hubert is shy and probably felt embarrassed to have the new student's attention focused on him.

19. D

A yo-yo is a toy that is made of two thick disks that are connected in the centre by a pin to which a string is attached.

20. D

Mr. Donaldson refers to the bathroom as "the facilities."

21. C

An exclamation mark is a punctuation mark that indicates that the speaker is making an exclamation, usually in excitement or shock.

22. D

A simile is a comparison between two objects using the words *like* or *as*. The phrase "'Taking Billie's backpack would be like ripping a shell off a turtle'" is a simile comparing Billie's backpack to a turtle's shell.

23. B

Billie talks about Alyssa "trying, as usual, to barge in where she's not wanted," and mentions wanting to make Alyssa disappear from her life. This indicates that Billie probably finds Alyssa annoying.

24. A

Josh asks Mr. Donaldson a lot of questions.

25. C

The word "especially" has four syllables: es•pe•cial•ly.

26. B

An excursion is a short trip or outing to some place.

27. A

A "reconstruction" is something that has been rebuilt or repaired to be as it was in the past, based on available information about its design and characteristics.

28. D

The correct sequence of events is listed in alternative **D**.

29. C

Hubert waits for Jean-Pierre after class.

30. B

Most kids probably feel nervous or scared when they first attend a new school.

31. D

The word "prophet" describes someone who predicts the future or receives information about the future from God. Without context clues, the reader would be using prior knowledge to recognize the meaning.

32. D

Evidence from the passage suggests that Stink is most likely Judy's little brother.

33. D

Judy put the fattest dictionary from her mom's office under her pillow. She knows that the dictionary is the information source for correct spelling.

34. D

The reader is asked to recall an important point. Judy wants to get "110%—zero-wrong-plus-extra-credit." (lines 39–40)

35. B

The question paraphrases information given in the passage. Mr. Todd gives tricorn-hat stickers to praise good work: "For once, she, Judy Moody, not Jessica (Flunk) Finch, would get a Thomas Jefferson tricorn-hat sticker for *Great Job, Good Thinking*."

36. C

The reader is able to discuss the main character and her feelings. Judy is feeling confident and sure of herself because she believes that she will wake up in the morning knowing all the spelling words.

37. D

The reader is able to infer "heavy" by using the context clue, "The fattest dictionary in the Moody house." (lines 25–26) The word lug means to pull with effort. Judy had to lug the dictionary, which implies that it was quite heavy.

38. A

The reader will explain connections between events and the main character. Judy is excited about not having to study for the spelling test, which indicates that she usually has to study quite hard for them. Her dream is to score 110%, which means that she probably does not usually score that high.

39. A

Judy uses the word "rare." When she is excited about the story of the Sleeping Prophet she says " 'When he woke up, he knew every word in the book. RARE!' " (line 10) In this question, the reader can confirm their understanding based on information in the text.

40. D

This question requires the reader to locate information. After putting the dictionary under her pillow, Judy "got into her cozy bowling-ball pajamas." (line 31)

41. D

The most appropriate option to the actual title would be Alternative D as the poem is about a vet who reignites a dragon's flame and, but for his flame-proof suit, would have been scorched by the dragon in return for efforts.

42. B

A simile is a figure of speech that compares two different things, usually in a phrase using the words "like" or "as."

43. D

The phrase "flicker of flame flashed" is an example of alliteration, which is the repetition of a letter or sound in two or more words that are closely associated.

44. A

A synonym for the word "gushed" is "poured."

45. C

According to the poem, the vet was "clutching a diamond the size of a star".

46. B

The word gi•gan•tic has three syllables.

47. A

The poem was clearly written to entertain the reader, it was not intended as a factual piece of information.

48. D

The group of words in alternative D is in alphabetical order.

49. D

As the dragon hunts "in the dark," it can be inferred that he hunts at night.

50. C

The vet "laughed at the brute/ because he was wearing his flame-proof suit."

51. D

Petrol is another word for gasoline.

52. C

The line "I see you've arrived" is in quotation marks because the dragon is speaking to the vet.

53. B

The dragon wanted the vet to come and see him because his flame had "gone out."

54. D

As the dragon is initially friendly, but then tries to burn the vet, the vet most likely finds the dragon unreliable.

UNIT TEST—READING

Read the following passage to answer questions 1 to 15.

Madame Love Doctor
from **All Because of a Cup of Coffee**

I reached the tenth floor, out of breath. My heart was beating wildly in my chest. A sign on the door in front of me read, *Madame Love Doctor.* Suddenly, it all became clear. My sister was sending me to a fortune-teller. Yes, some wacky mouse who claims to tell
5 the future. I groaned. I didn't have time for this mumbo jumbo. I had my whole day planned out. First I would feel sorry for myself. Then I would cry me a river of tears. Then I would float him and cry some more. Yes, I had an important schedule to keep.

I was about to leave when the door opened with a creak.
10 I caught sight of a dusty room. It smelled like incense and burning candles.

"Come in," said a feeble voice. "I've been waiting for you."

How strange, I thought. I could have sworn I had heard that voice before. But before I could figure it out, the voice continued.
15 "Come in, Mr. Stilton," it murmured. "And bring your broken little heart with you.

I froze. How did she know my name? And how did she know about the countess?

In the corner of the room, I saw a strange figure. She was
20 wearing a long, flowing dress. Her head was covered by a faded pawkerchief. The room was so dark, I couldn't make out her face.

The fortune-teller pushed me into a chair. Then she uncovered a crystal ball. I almost giggled. Maybe next she would try to read the lines on my paw. It was all so very silly. I wanted to
25 leave, but right then, the fortune-teller began to whisper.

"I see roses. A whole van of roses," she murmured. "And chocolates. Gourmet cheese-flavored chocolates. Yum, yum."

"Roses aren't enough, neither are chocolates," she went on. "You need much more to win over this mouse, Germeister."

30   I blinked. "Germeister?" I murmured. How very strange. Why did this rodent seem sooo familiar to me?

She coughed, then continued. "Are you willing to do anything to make your true love fall at your paws?" she asked.

Hope made my heart beat faster. I nodded "yes" so hard that
35 my eyes rattled in my fur. I leaned closer.

The fortune-teller told me I needed to do something extraordinary. Something no mouse had ever done before. Something so amazing it would make me famouse. Then Stephanie von Sugarfur would be sure to notice me.

40   I scratched my head. "S-S-Something amazing?" I stammered. "But I'm just an average mouse. I run a newspaper. I'm not an explorer."

The fortune-teller took a closer look at her crystal ball. "But I see that some very clever rodents want you to go on a trip with
45 them. You must go. It will be an amazing success!" She predicted.

I chewed my whiskers. I was planning on sulking in front of the TV set all weekend. Still, my family would be so happy if I joined them on their trip.

"Do you really think it will work?" I asked.

50   "Of course, you cheesebrain!" she shrieked. "Madame Love Doctor knows all. Now go home, pack your suitcase, and be off!

Then she held out her fleshy paw. "By the way, that will be two hundred dollars."

My jaw hit the ground. My blood ran cold. My fur stood up in
55 shock. Did this rodent really have magical powers?

The fortune-teller sniggered with delight. I guess she liked surprising her clients.

I nearly fell off my chair. Two hundred dollars! What a business. Maybe I should buy my own crystal ball. I could be rich!
60 As if in a dream, I took out my wallet. Quicker than a cat with a ball of yarn, she snatched up the cash.

I headed out the door.

"And don't forget to play it cool!" the fortune-teller called after me. I stopped. Now, where had I heard those words recently?
65 Before I could remember, a paw grabbed my shoulder. It was Thea.

"How did it go?" she asked.

I told her what the fortune-teller had said. About the roses. About the chocolates. And about the amazing trip that would make me famouse. "So I will go with you," I finished.

70   For some reason, Thea didn't look too surprised. We roared off on her bike.

"Hang on to your whiskers!" my sister cried.

I was hanging on to more than my whiskers. I was hanging on for dear life!

—*by* Geronimo Stilton

1. Mr. Stilton was most likely out of breath when he reached the tenth floor because he

   A. had allergies

   B. just woke up

   C. was very excited

   D. walked up a lot of stairs

2. A fortune teller is a person who

   A. tells people where they should go

   B. predicts other people's futures

   C. gives money to other people

   D. teaches people about luck

3. Mr. Stilton most likely almost giggled when the fortune-teller uncovered a crystal ball because he

   A. thought the room was full of interesting objects

   B. does not believe that people can tell the future

   C. wanted the lady to think he was friendly

   D. thought of a really funny joke

4. How many syllables are in the word extraordinary?

   A. Four

   B. Five

   C. Six

   D. Seven

5. Which of the following groups of words are in alphabetical order?

   A. Sulking, success, suitcase, sure

   B. Sure, suitcase, sulking, success

   C. Suitcase, sure, success, sulking

   D. Success, suitcase, sulking, sure

6. The word "extraordinary" refers to something

   A. special

   B. magical

   C. common

   D. impossible

7. The writer most likely wrote this story to

   A. let the reader enjoy a silly tale

   B. describe what it is like to be a mouse

   C. convince the reader to become a fortune-teller

   D. give the reader information about falling in love

8. At the beginning of the passage, Mr. Stilton most likely thinks that the fortune-teller is

   A. odd

   B. tired

   C. kind

   D. lonely

9. In the passage, the writer put the line, "Do you really think it will work?" in quotation marks because

   A. someone was asking a question

   B. a character was whispering

   C. a character was speaking

   D. someone was yelling

10. What had Mr. Stilton planned to do all weekend before going to the fortune-teller?

    A. Sulk in front of the TV

    B. Chew on his whiskers

    C. Go on a trip

    D. Eat cheese

11. When Mr. Stilton is riding on Thea's bike and "hanging on for dear life," he most likely feels

    A. bored

    B. scared

    C. pleased

    D. confused

12. In the phrase, "the amazing trip that would make me famouse," (lines 68–69) the word "amazing" means

   A. frightening

   B. wonderful

   C. boring

   D. long

13. Mr. Stilton is in love with

   A. the fortune-teller

   B. an explorer

   C. Stephanie

   D. Thea

14. Which of the following lists shows the order of events as they actually happened in the story?

   A. Mr. Stilton saw a dusty room; Thea and Mr. Stilton roared off on her bike; the fortune-teller uncovered a crystal ball; the fortune teller told Mr. Stilton he needed to do something extraordinary.

   B. Thea and Mr. Stilton roared off on her bike; the fortune-teller uncovered a crystal ball; Mr. Stilton saw a dusty room; the fortune-teller told Mr. Stilton he needed to do something extraordinary.

   C. The fortune-teller uncovered a crystal ball; the fortune-teller told Mr. Stilton he needed to do something extraordinary; Mr. Stilton saw a dusty room; Thea and Mr. Stilton roared off on her bike.

   D. Mr. Stilton saw a dusty room; the fortune-teller uncovered a crystal ball; the fortune-teller told Mr. Stilton he needed to do something extraordinary; Thea and Mr. Stilton roared off on her bike.

15. This passage can best be described as a

   A. mystery

   B. folklore

   C. fantasy

   D. poem

Read the following passage to answer questions 16 to 21.

Weather and Climate

How are snowflakes made? If the air in a cloud is below freezing (0°C), some of the water vapour freezes into ice crystals, these ice crystals then stick together to make snowflakes. The temperature and amount of water in a cloud affects the shape of a snowflake. For example, when
5   the temperature is very cold and the cloud is very moist, needle-shaped flakes form, whereas, if the temperature is warm, star shape snowflakes form. Each snowflake has a completely different shape but they all have six points.

Snowflakes can be heavy enough that they fall out of the cloud as
10   snow. Heavy snow often builds up behind barriers like fences or walls to create snowdrifts. Small animals can move around easily in tunnels under snow and it keeps them warm like a blanket on a bed.

16. Snowflakes are made up of

    A. water droplets

    B. ice crystals

    C. hailstones

    D. icicles

17. Snowflakes can be shaped like

    A. balls or stars

    B. needles or stars

    C. circles or squares

    D. crystals or droplets

18. The reason that small animals like to tunnel under the snow is that

    A. it is warmer under the snow

    B. they cannot dig out of the snow

    C. it gives them a shortcut to get to places

    D. they are not good at running on top of the snow

19. Every snowflake has

    A. four points

    B. six points

    C. eight points

    D. ten points

20. A snowdrift can be best described as

 A. a snowstorm

 B. a pile of snow

 C. blowing snowflakes

 D. a cloud that forms snow

21. In the phrase, "Needle-shaped flakes form in very cold moist air," (line 5) the word "moist" means

 A. dry

 B. wet

 C. cold

 D. warm

ANSWERS AND SOLUTIONS—UNIT TEST

1. D	6. A	11. B	16. B	21. B
2. B	7. A	12. B	17. B	
3. B	8. A	13. C	18. A	
4. C	9. C	14. D	19. B	
5. D	10. A	15. C	20. B	

1. D

Mr. Stilton was most likely out of breath because he just "reached the tenth floor." The implication is that the mouse walked up ten flights of stairs, and that would take a lot of energy.

2. B

A fortune-teller is a person who makes predictions about another person's future, usually by looking into a crystal ball, reading palms, or using tarot cards.

3. B

Mr. Stilton almost laughed when he saw the crystal ball because he does not believe that fortune-tellers are actually able to see the future. This is evident in the next line: "Maybe next she would try to read the lines on my paw." Clearly, he is skeptical of the fortune-teller's abilities.

4. C

The word ex•tra•or•di•nar•y has six syllables.

5. D

The words "Success, suitcase, sulking, sure" are in alphabetical order.

6. A

The word extraordinary means special or strange.

7. A

Since the story does not have any clear educational purpose, we can assume that the author wrote this fantastical tale to entertain the reader.

8. A

At the beginning of the passage, Mr. Stilton refers to the fortune-teller as "some wacky mouse," and that he "saw a strange figure" who was "wearing a long flowing dress" with a faded "pawkerchief" covering her head.

9. C

Quotation marks are used to enclose what someone is saying, regardless of *how* they are saying it.

10. A

Before visiting the fortune-teller, Mr. Stilton was "planning on sulking in front of the TV set all weekend."

11. B

When Mr. Stilton is on Thea's bike he is "hanging on for dear life." This implies that he is feeling frightened or scared.

12. B

The word amazing means astonishing, remarkable, or wonderful.

13. C

Mr. Stilton wants to do "something so amazing it would make me famouse. Then Stephanie von Sugarfur would be sure to notice me."

14. D

The events listed in alternative **D** are in chronological order.

15. C

This type of story is a fantasy because it is a fiction featuring a magical world.

16. B

Snowflakes are made of ice crystals. "If the air in a cloud is below freezing, or 32°F (0°C), some of the water vapor freezes into ice crystals instead of forming water droplets. These crystals stick together to make snowflakes." (Lines 1–3)

17. B

Snowflakes can be shaped like needles or stars: "The shape of a snowflake depends on the temperature and the amount of water in a cloud. Needle-shaped flakes form in very cold moist air, while star shapes form in warmer air." (Lines 5–6)

18. A

Snow traps warmth underneath it, like a comforter on a bed. Small animals can keep warm in winter by tunneling under the snow.

19. B

Every snowflake has six points, but different shapes of crystals can form on those points.

20. B

A snowdrift is a mound or pile of snow.

21. B

The word "moist" means that something is wet or damp.

NOTES

Writing

NOTES

WRITING STRATEGIES

2.4.3.1 *Experiment with a variety of story beginnings to choose one that best introduces particular stories*

OFF TO A GOOD START

The beginning of a story sets the stage for everything that follows. A good beginning captures the reader's attention and draws him in, making him want to read more. Read the following story beginnings and imagine what their stories might be about. Which one is most likely to begin a mystery story? Could one start a funny story? What about a fairy tale?

- Once upon a time, in a land of castles and dragons…
- I thought I was heading off for just another boring day of school. Little did I know how wrong I was.
- Gemma was a child of the night.
- The way I see it, there are families and then there's my family. They are really two different things altogether.
- The house at the bottom of Chestnut Street had been empty for as long as anyone could remember.

Although the first sentences of a story are the first thing the reader sees, they are often not the first thing a writer will write. It is a good idea to check your beginning after you have finished your story. Experiment with different beginnings to see how they change the feel of a story.

2.4.4.1 *Use sentence variety to link ideas and create impressions on familiar audiences*

ADDING VARIETY TO YOUR SENTENCES

If too many sentences are the same length and have the same basic structure, writing becomes boring to read. Using different types and lengths of sentences is called writing with *sentence variety*. Notice how the sentences in the first example are very similar. They are quite short, and almost all are simple sentences. Most start with the main noun *I*, *they*, *it*, or *we*, followed by the verb. In the second example, the sentence beginnings vary. Connecting words such as *when*, *since*, and *and* make the ideas flow together better.

The following example shows how usings connecting words makes your writing better.

First Version

I went to school yesterday. I met up with my friend on the way there. His name is Jude. We found a puppy. It was crying. It seemed to be lost. Jude checked its tag. There was a phone number on it. We took the puppy to the school office. I phoned the owners. They were very happy to hear that we had found their dog. They rushed over to get him. They were happy to see each other.

New Version

Yesterday, I met up with my friend Jude on the way to school. We were almost there when we came across the cutest little puppy I have ever seen. It cried so pitifully, we thought it must be lost. Jude, who has a dog of his own, knew to check the puppy's tag for a phone number. Since we were almost at school, I picked the little thing up and carried it to the office. When we phoned the owners, they were thrilled to hear that we had found their dog and rushed straight over to get him. It was a very happy reunion!

3.2.1.1   *Find information to answer research questions using a variety of sources, such as children's magazines, CDROMs, plays, folk tales, songs, stories and the environment*

3.1.1.2   *Identify facts and opinions, main ideas and details in oral, print and other media texts*

3.2.2.2   *Locate answers to questions and extract appropriate and significant information from oral, print and other media texts*

3.2.3.1   *Review information to determine its usefulness in answering research questions*

3.3.3.1   *Determine if gathered information is sufficient to answer research questions*

3.3.1.1   *Organize ideas and information, using a variety of strategies, such as clustering, categorizing and sequencing*

3.3.2.1   *Record facts and ideas using a variety of strategies; list titles and authors of sources*

RESEARCHING TOPICS

The process of gathering information about a subject is called research. People research for many reasons: to complete a school project or report, plan a vacation, decide what camera to buy, or learn more about a topic of interest. When you are conducting research, you should use a variety of sources.

Using a wide range of sources will help ensure that you have as much information as possible to choose from. Examples of sources include

- Printed material—encyclopaedias, textbooks, magazines, fiction or information books specific to your subject matter
- Electronic media—Internet, CDs or DVDs, audio recordings
- People—experts in the area you are studying, people with relevant personal experience

FACTS AND OPINIONS

When you are reading to learn new things or find information for a report, it is important that you can tell the difference between facts and opinions.

Facts are things that are true and can be proven. The following are all facts:

- Alberta is a province in Canada.
- The sky is blue today.
- Many young Albertans play hockey every winter.
- Sweet peas are climbing flowers that have a strong scent.
- James is the fastest runner on the track team.

Opinions, on the other hand, are what someone thinks or feels about something. Often, an opinion uses the words *feel*, *believe*, or *think*, but other times these words are left out. The following are examples of opinions:

- Alberta is the best province in Canada.
- I think the blue of a summer sky is the happiest colour in the world.
- Hockey is the best sport to play in an Alberta winter.
- Sweet peas are climbing flowers that look beautiful and smell great.
- I feel that James should receive an award for being such a good athlete.

Opinions can be interesting and even helpful, but they should not be confused with facts. If you include opinions in a report, you should always clearly show that they are opinions. For example, if you were writing a report on winter sports in Alberta, you could say that hockey is "your favourite" sport or that "many people think" hockey is the best winter sport. It would not be appropriate to say that hockey is the best sport or the coolest sport or the most boring sport, unless you added the words "in my opinion," "I think," or something else that sets the statement apart from the facts. See if you can tell which of the following sentences are facts and which are opinions:

- Science class is very cool these days.
- We are learning about how buildings are designed and made.
- Nathan's dad is an architect, and he came to talk to us about an office building he designed.
- He has the best job in the whole world!

RECORDING AND ORGANIZING INFORMATION

Once you have gathered the sources you plan to use, your next step is to find the information that will be most useful to you. Using the reading strategies from the beginning of this book, make note of the facts as you come across them. You have probably learned to make jot notes of your information. Jot notes are words or phrases that you write down to help you remember important facts that you have read. Do not try to write down all the words you read. You should not be using complete sentences for your jot notes. For example, if you read the following sentence,

"The blue whale is the largest animal on Earth, weighing as much as 180 metric tonnes and measuring up to 33 metres in length."

ou might make jot notes that look like this:

- Blue whale
  - world's largest animal
  - up to 180 tonnes
  - up to 33 metres long

There are many ways to organize your jot notes. One of the most effective ways is to put your information into a diagram. Here are some diagrams, called graphic organizers, that you could use. The one you choose will depend on the type of research you are doing.

Sequence

Events are organized in the order in which they occur. Examples are recipes and science experiments, which follow a logical order:

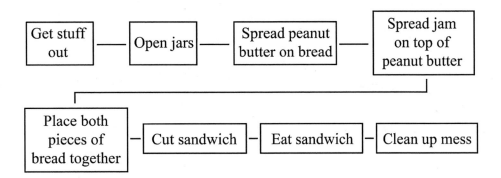

Compare/Contrast

Information is organized according to the *similarities* and *differences* of two or more topics:

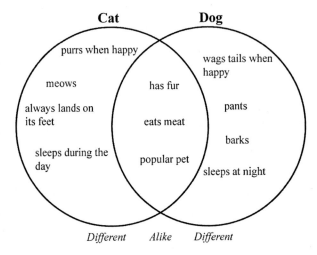

Web

A web is useful for sorting facts about a topic. We saw this web earlier in the book with the passage "Giants of the Forest." A web is a good way to see your main topic surrounded by all the details (facts) that support it.

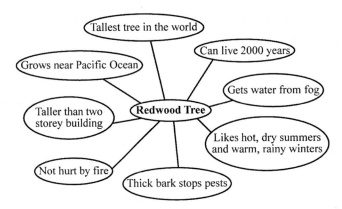

REVIEWING INFORMATION

Once you have gathered your facts together, it is good to review them to make sure you have enough information to meet your needs. Look back at why you were doing the research in the first place. Did your teacher assign you a topic? Were you curious about a subject and wanted to know more?

Let's say your teacher asked you to write a report about Redwood trees. In reviewing your facts, you realize that you do not know if Redwoods are endangered. Although you determined during your research that fire and pests do not hurt Redwoods, you do not know if the Redwood habitat is threatened by logging. You may need to do additional research to answer this question.

Where Did Your Facts Come From?

Many people forget to keep track of the sources they used to find the information they need. This is an important step in research, especially now that so many people do research on the Internet. You might be able to remember the title of a book you took out of the school library, but will you remember the address for every website you visited? Keep a list of all the sources you use. For example, if you were writing a report on wolves, you might note that you had used the following sources:

- *Wolf: Legend, Enemy, Icon*, by Rebecca Grambo (book)
- "Wolf," from kids.nationalgeographic.com (video on the Internet)
- "What's in a Howl," by Fred Harrington (article and audio clip from www.pbs.org)

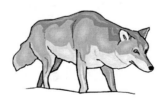

4.2.2.1   *use phonic knowledge and skills and visual memory, systematically, to spell phonically regular, three-syllable words in own writing*

4.2.2.2   *identify generalizations that assist with the spelling of unfamiliar words, including irregular plurals in own writing*

4.2.2.3   *identify misspelled words, develop strategies for learning to spell them correctly in own writing*

WRITING AND SPELLING WORDS

Now that you have some strategies for improving your understanding of words, your spelling will also improve. The more attention you pay to a word, its meaning, how it is built of a root word, and any prefixes and suffixes, the more likely you will be to remember how to spell it. That is more fun and interesting than studying spelling lists! The next time your parents tell you not to read under the covers after lights-out, you can honestly say, "but Mom, I'm just working on my spelling!"

There are many other things that will help you to spell better while you are writing. Breaking words into parts (root, prefix, and suffix) and syllables will help you to spell them correctly. Sounding words out in your head as you write will also help your spelling. Most experts seem to agree that the best thing to do when writing is to get your ideas down on paper quickly without worrying too much about spelling. You should then go back over what you have written and circle or highlight any words that do not look right. Many students find it much easier to identify misspelled words when reading them than when actually writing them. Once you have circled the words that you are worried about, you can check with a friend, teacher, or dictionary to confirm the spelling and revise your writing.

When you read, you will come across many of the same spelling patterns again and again. Make note of these patterns as you read. These patterns can help you spell words that you already know and help you to learn new words.

In English, there are many spelling patterns. Knowing these patterns can help you to spell. Unfortunately there are also many words that do not follow the patterns. These words you will just end up learning over time. Following are some examples of spelling patterns that you may already know:

- *i* before *e* except after *c*
  bel**ie**ve   rec**ei**ve
- *qu* (*q* is almost always followed by *u*)
  quack   **qu**ake
- *ea* can have three different sounds: a short *e* sound (as in bread), a long *a* sound (as in *break*), or a long *e* sound (as in *read*)

Short *e*	Long *a*	Long *e*
dead	great	read
bread	break	bead
instead		dream
head		beat
heaven		cream

RHYMING WORDS

Words that rhyme often share the same spelling rules, but not always.
If you know how to spell one word, you may be able to work out rhyming words. Notice in the following table that all the words in a column rhyme with the top word. The last two, however, follow different spelling rules.

	tree	**itch**	**gate**	**been**	**cry**	**right**
same spelling	three	pitch	late	queen	sky	might
same spelling	see	witch	date	green	why	night
same spelling	bee	stitch	plate	seen	dry	bright
different spelling	*she*	*which*	*eight*	*mean*	*high*	*white*
different spelling	*key*	*rich*	*great*	*machine*	*pie*	*bite*

BUILDING WORDS WITH PREFIXES AND SUFFIXES

English words can have three parts: the root word, the prefix, and the suffix. The basic meaning of the word is the root word. Root words are complete words on their own. Prefixes and suffixes are groups of letters that are added to some root words. When a prefix or suffix is added, the meaning of the root word changes.

A prefix is attached to the beginning of a root word to change its meaning. Each prefix has its own meaning:

- *re-* means *again*
  rewrite = write again
  *re*tell = tell again
- *un-* means *not*
  unhappy = not happy
  unhelpful = not helpful

A suffix is added to the end of a root word to change its meaning:

- *-ed* changes a verb from present to past tense
  walk + ed = walk**ed**
- *-ful* means *full of* or *with*
  help**ful** = full of help
  peace**ful** = full of peace
- *-less* means *without*
  home**less** = without a home
  taste**less** = without taste

Sometimes, the root word changes a bit when a suffix is added. Watch out for these words in your writing. The two main rules are worth reviewing:

Letters are sometimes doubled when a suffix is added. This is so that the vowel remains a short vowel. If the letter were not doubled, the vowel would be pronounced incorrectly as a long vowel:

- run + ing = run**ning** (*n* is doubled)
- bat + er = bat**ter** (*t* is doubled)

Sometimes a final letter is dropped from the root word when a suffix is added. For example, when the suffix *-ing* is added to words that end in *e*, the root word also changes. The *e* at the end of the word is dropped and then *-ing* is added:

- choose + ing = choos**ing** (*e* is dropped)
- piano + ist = pian**ist** (*o* is dropped)

PLURALS

Some nouns are singular, meaning that they describe one thing. Other words are plural, meaning that they describe more than one thing. For example, the word *banana* is singular and the word *bananas* is plural. We call plurals that follow one of the common rules "Regular Plurals" and the others "Irregular Plurals."

Regular Plurals

1. Usually, add *s* to the singular word.

dog	becomes	dogs
tree	becomes	trees
ball	becomes	balls

2. Add *-es* when the word ends in *s*, *x*, *z*, *ch*, or *sh*.

bus	becomes	buses
fox	becomes	foxes
lunch	becomes	lunches
bush	becomes	bushes

3. When a word ends with a consonant and a *y*, change the *y* to *i* and add *-es*.

cherry	becomes	cherries
penny	become	pennies

4. When a word ends in *f* or *fe*, change the *f* to *v* and add *-es*.

wolf	becomes	wolves
leaf	becomes	leaves
life	becomes	lives

Irregular Plurals

5. Some words need to be changed at their roots to become plural. These are called irregular plurals.

1 mouse	becomes	2 mice
1 tooth	becomes	15 teeth
1 man	becomes	4 men
1 goose	becomes	10 geese

6. Some words stay the same whether or not they are plural.

1 sheep	is the same for	2 sheep
1 deer	is the same for	15 deer
1 fish	is the same for	4 fish
1 moose	is the same for	10 moose

One Sheep

Two Sheep

4.1.4.1 *Explain relationships among words and concepts associated with topics of study*

HOW WORDS ARE RELATED

One way to increase your vocabulary (the number of words you know) is to read about many different subjects. Many words are used mostly in certain subject areas. For example, if you are reading or writing about computers, you would probably come across words like *keyboard*, *laptop*, *mouse pad*, *website*, *email*, *online*, and *memory* and acronyms like CPU and CDROM. If you were reading about gardening, you would find a completely different variety of words, such as *rake*, *weeds*, *spades*, *transplant*, and *seedling*. If you were writing about the sport of basketball, you would probably use words like *rebound*, *lay-up*, *referee*, *slam-dunk*, *foul*, *forward*, and *court*.

Here are a couple of exercises you can do with a friend to help build your vocabulary in specific subject areas:

1. Take turns picking a subject. It can be just about anything that pops into your head. Each of you write six to eight words that you think would be used when writing about that subject. When you have finished, compare your lists.
   - How many of the words were the same?
   - Did your friend have any words you did not know?
   - Check each other's spelling and if there are words you are unsure about and need to look up in a dictionary.

Decide whether or not any words can be used for other subjects. For instance, the word *court* is used in many different sports besides basketball, and may also be used in the context of a law court or a royal court.

2. Take turns picking a subject. Each find a short article from a magazine, encyclopaedia, or website that talks about that subject. Each write down six to eight words you find in that article that you think are specific to that subject. When you have finished, compare your lists.
   - How many of the words were the same?
   - If they were very different, why do you think that was? Were the articles quite different? For example, if your subject was ladybugs, perhaps one article was more about how ladybugs behave, while the other was more about where ladybugs live.
   - Have your friend explain the meaning of any words on her list that you do not know and do the same for her with your words.

Following are a few subjects you could use to get started:

- beehives
- ballet
- stormy weather
- mathematics
- going camping
- being sick with a cold

4.1.4.2 *Experiment with words and word meanings to produce a variety of effects*

EXPERIMENTING WITH WORDS

Writing is all about choosing words that make your ideas clear to someone else. Sometimes, there are different words that mean the same thing but are more interesting, fun, or exciting. For instance, if you are telling someone about a book you have read, you could simply write that it was a *good* book. It would be more interesting and useful to the reader if you wrote whether it was exciting, hilarious, well-written, fascinating, or surprising.

Some words have a nice sound to them, like *hullaballoo, gurgle, frazzled, flip-flop, squishy, dandelion,* and *hippopotamus.* Do you have any favourite words? Why do you like them? Try to find a way to use one of your favourite words every day for the next week. Challenge your family and friends to do the same thing. It will probably produce some giggles for all of you!

Some words sound interesting or funny with other words, such as *Anna Banana, creepy crawly,* and *giggling gaggle of girls.*

Other words sound like the thing they describe, such as *buzz, whoosh, boing,* or *creak.*

Read the following lines from a poem:
Slippery, sliding, slithery snake,
Wrapped around a rusty rake...

Why do you think the poet chose the words she did? See if you can find any sounds that repeat? Are there any rhymes? Are there words that sound like the things they describe?

4.2.1.3   *Use adjectives and adverbs to add interest and detail in own writing*

SPICE UP YOUR WRITING WITH ADJECTIVES AND ADVERBS

Adjectives and adverbs can be your very best friends when it comes to making your writing more interesting. Adjectives are words that describe nouns, and adverbs are words that describe verbs. Read the following examples and see if you can add some more.

Noun	Adjectives that might describe the noun
bicycle	shiny, fast, new, blue, fancy, cool, second-hand, rusty
dog	fluffy, sleek, muscular, yappy, gruff, scary, gentle, friendly, energetic
dancer	beautiful, graceful, flexible, strong, talented, groovy, radical, wild
tree	
game	
movie	

Verb	Adverbs that might describe the verb
ran	quickly, noisily, carefully, swiftly, gracefully, suddenly
talks	quickly, harshly, quietly, softly, gently, constantly, grumpily
stomped	wildly, noisily, angrily, carelessly, clumsily
played	
rolling	
waited	

As you write, ask yourself if the adjectives and adverbs you choose are the best for what you are describing. Do they really mean exactly what you want to say? If not, try using a thesaurus to look up other words that have similar meanings (synonyms). The next time you find yourself using dull words like *big, nice,* or *good,* try changing them for something with a little more spice!

4.1.5.1 *Choose words, language patterns, illustrations or sounds to add detail and create desired effects in oral, print and other media texts*

ADDING DETAIL

Whether you are writing, telling, or even acting out a story, your job is to make it interesting and engaging for your audience. If you are writing a poem or a story, perhaps you will choose to add pictures to enhance your words. Perhaps you will choose to print some words differently to make them stand out. The actual words you choose can make a big difference to your writing. They can change a story from serious to funny or from slow to exciting.

One way to practise creative writing and storytelling is to take a story you already know well and change it. Here are a few examples:

1. How would the fairy tale *Cinderella* change if the main character were a boy called Cinderino? What if he lived in a city in the present day?
2. How would the story *Goldilocks and the Three Bears* be different if it were changed to *Goldifur and the Three People*?
3. What would have happened if the superhero Spiderman had been bitten by a radioactive snake instead of a spider? What would his superhero name be and what kind of powers would he have?

4.2.1.1 *Identify a variety of sentence types, and use in own writing*

TYPES OF SENTENCES

All sentences must have at least one subject, one verb, and express a complete idea, but they can be a lot more complicated than that. We do not generally speak using all complete sentences, but it is important to learn how to write good, complete, and interesting sentences to make your meaning clear. The most basic sentences are known as simple sentences. A simple sentence may have more than one subject, but it only has one verb idea. Note that a verb idea might be more than one actual word, such as in *had lived, could have had,* or *must have been.* Following are some examples of simple sentences. In each sentence, the subject has been bolded and the verb idea underlined:

John <u>plays</u> soccer.
John and **Jacob** <u>play</u> soccer.
My brother John <u>plays</u> soccer.
John <u>has been playing</u> soccer for five years.
John and **his soccer team** <u>should have won</u> the finals this year.

In the examples, you can clearly see that each sentence has one verb idea, although there may be more than one subject. When two or more verb ideas are linked in a sentence, it becomes a compound sentence. Following are some examples of compound sentences. Again, you can clearly see the verb ideas underlined and the subjects in bold print:

John <u>plays</u> soccer in the summer and <u>skis</u> in the winter.
John <u>plays</u> soccer, but **I** <u>prefer</u> softball.
John <u>plays</u> soccer and **Jacob** <u>does</u> too.
On Tuesdays, **John** and **Jacob** <u>play</u> soccer and **I** <u>go</u> to swimming lessons.
John <u>played</u> soccer yesterday, but **Jacob** <u>did not</u>.

Sentences can look very different depending on what they are trying to say. There are four types of sentences that you will learn to write, although you do not necessarily need to remember what they are called at this point.

Declarative sentences make a statement:
    John's team won the soccer game.

Interrogative sentences ask a question:
    Did John's team win?

Imperative sentences command or order:
    Get out there and run your hardest!
    Don't touch the ball with your hands.

Exclamatory sentences show excitement:
    What a great game you played!

4.2.1.2 *Identify correct subject-verb agreement, and use in own writing*

MATCHING SUBJECT AND VERB

Every sentence must contain a noun subject and a verb used correctly together.

A verb must be in its correct form for the subject.

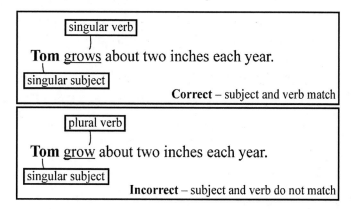

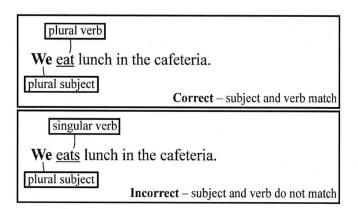

You can see from the examples that a singular subject must be matched with a singular verb, and a plural subject must be matched with a plural verb.

4.1.2.2   *Edit for complete and incomplete sentences*

4.2.1.4   *Distinguish between complete and incomplete sentences*

WHAT MAKES A SENTENCE COMPLETE?

When writing, the rule is that you should always use complete sentences, even though we do not always speak that way. If you are writing dialogue (direct speech) in a story, it would be acceptable to have the characters speak using some incomplete sentences, also called utterances. Let's review what makes a sentence complete. A sentence must have a noun subject and a matching verb. The very simplest complete sentence would have only these two things:

✓**Jane** <u>cried</u>.
✓**Jonah** <u>laughed</u>.

Most sentences have some other information to make the idea more clear or complete:

✓**Jane** <u>cried</u> because she skinned her knee.
✓**Jonah** <u>laughed</u> at the dog's tricks.

Sometimes, extra information can confuse you because the sentence looks long enough, but it still might be incomplete if the subject's verb is missing.
Look carefully at the following sentences:

✗**Jane,** my very best friend in the whole wide world.
✗On Tuesday, **Jonah**, the kid from next door.

The key thing to remember is that the statement must be finished for the sentence to be complete, even if it has a subject and a verb. Following are some unfinished ideas:

✗**Jane** <u>cried</u> because.
✗**Jane** <u>cried</u> because she skinned her.
✗**Jonah** <u>laughed</u> at the dog's.
✗**Jonah** <u>laughed</u> the dog's tricks.

Usually, you will notice that a sentence is incomplete when you read it to yourself because it sounds like something is missing:

       ✗**Jane** <u>cried </u>because. (Why did she cry?)

       ✗**Jane** <u>cried </u>because she skinned her. (What did she skin?)

Unfortunately, complete and incomplete sentences are a bit more complicated than that, but you will learn the trickier things as you get older. For the time being, the best thing you can do is read your own sentences after you have written them and ask yourself, "Is this is a complete idea or statement? Does anything feel like it got cut off in the middle?"

The following example is more complicated:

       ✗On Tuesday, Jonah, who lives next door.

There is a verb in this sentence (*lives*), but the sentence is still incomplete. The phrase "who lives next door" is together just extra information explaining who Jonah is. We still are left wondering, "What did Jonah do on Tuesday?" There needs to be a verb matching the subject:

       ✓On Tuesday, **Jonah**, who lives next door, <u>laughed</u> at the dog's tricks.

Now it is a complete statement. For now, it is not important for you to know the exact grammatical rules that make this sentence complete. Just get used to looking for the main noun subject and its matching verb and checking whether the statement or question feels complete and makes sense.

4.2.3.1 *Use capital letters appropriately in titles of books and stories*

4.2.3.2 *Use exclamation marks, appropriately, as end punctuation in own writing*

4.2.3.3 *Use apostrophes to form common contractions and to show possession in own writing*

4.2.3.4 *Identify commas, end punctuation, apostrophes and quotation marks when reading, and use them to assist comprehension*

PUNCTUATION

It is important to be able to correctly use periods, question marks, exclamation marks, commas, apostrophes, and quotation marks.

There are a lot of punctuation rules that you do not need to know yet. Whole big books have been written about all the punctuation rules. Do not worry too much about all the rules yet. Here are the basic things expected of Grade 3 students:

1. You should know when to use the three types of ending punctuation and be able to say why a writer might have chosen one over another:

.	Period—use at the end of a sentence that tells something or makes a command: *Yesterday I walked to school.*
?	Question mark—use at the end of a sentence that asks a question: *How did you get to school yesterday?*
!	Exclamation mark—use at the end of a sentence that shows excitement: *I can't believe you walked to school through that snow!*

2. You should also know how to use the following punctuation:

> Comma—between words or expressions that are in a list
> or a series:
>
> *She picked blueberries, raspberries, cherries, and
> apples for her pie.*

3. You should also know how to use apostrophes in two ways:

> Apostrophe—use to show belonging:
> *The girl's dog was black.*
>
> Apostrophe—use to take the place of letters left out in contractions
> (two words made into one word by leaving out letters):
>
> | Two Words | Contraction |
> |---|---|
> | we have | we've |
> | you will | you'll |
> | it is | it's |
> | she is | she's |
> | should not | shouldn't |
> | there is | there's |
>
> Here is the trickiest thing to remember—the difference between *it's*
> and *its*:
>
> It's got its own rule:
>
> *The dog ate its supper.* (its= belonging to it)
> *It's a hot day outside.* (it's = it is)

4. You should know how to use quotation marks in three different ways:

> Quotation marks—use to show dialogue (speaking), quotations, and titles of short stories, poems, songs, and articles. Quotation marks always come in pairs:
>
> *"I will get you for this!" he shouted after her.* (dialogue)
>
> *In her article on the power of music, the author said, "music has the strength to make you cry, laugh, fight, or love."* (quotation)
>
> *One of my favourite poems is "Alligator Pie."*
> (title of poem)

CAPITAL LETTERS

There are four big rules about when to use CAPITAL letters:

1. Use a capital letter at the beginning of a sentence:
   The fox jumped over the log.
2. Use a capital letter for the word *I*:
   He and I went to the park.
3. Use a capital letter for the first letter of important words in a title:
   Charlie and the Chocolate Factory
4. Use a capital letter to begin names of people, places, and things. These are also called proper nouns:
   Sam, March, Calgary

KEY *Strategies for Success on Tests*

NOTES

 # AN OVERVIEW OF THE TEST

This section is all about the skills and strategies you need to be successful on the Provincial Achievement Test for Grade 3 English Language Arts. It is designed for you to use together with your classroom learning and assignments.

FINDING OUT ABOUT THE TEST

Here are some questions you may wish to discuss with your teacher to help you prepare for Part B of the Provincial Achievement Test for Grade 3 English Language Arts:

1.	What is the purpose of the test?	The purpose is to see how well you construct meaning, reflect on reading, and understand what you read.
2.	What do I need to know to do well on the assessment?	By the end of Grade 3 you are expected to actively make meaning by understanding explicitly stated information and ideas; understand implicitly stated information (make inferences) and respond to reading by making connections between text information and personal knowledge.
3.	What must I bring for the test?	You must bring a pencil and an eraser.
4.	Will there be graphics?	Yes, diagrams, pictures, and illustrations.
5.	What kinds of questions are on the test?	There will be multiple-choice on the test.
6.	How many types of each question are there?	There are 40 multiple choice questions.
7.	How important is this test to my final grade?	Your teacher can answer this question.

Having a good understanding of effective test taking skills can help your performance on the test. Being familiar with the question format may help you in preparing for quizzes, unit tests or year-end assessments.

TEST PREPARATION AND TEST-TAKING SKILLS

THINGS TO CONSIDER WHEN TAKING A TEST

✓ It is normal to feel anxious before you write a test. You can manage this anxiety by:
  - thinking positive thoughts. Visual imagery is a helpful technique to try.
  - making a conscious effort to relax by taking several slow, controlled, deep breaths. Concentrate on the air going in and out of the body.

✓ Before you begin the test, ask questions if you are unsure of anything.

✓ Jot down key words or phrases from any oral directions.

✓ Look over the entire test to assess the number and kinds of questions on the test.

✓ Read each question closely and reread if necessary.

✓ Pay close attention to key vocabulary words. Sometimes, these are bolded or italicized, and they are usually important words in the question.

✓ Mark your answers on your answer sheet carefully. If you wish to change an answer, erase the mark and then ensure that your final answer is darker than the one that you have erased.

✓ On the test booklet, use highlighting to note directions, key words and vocabulary that you find confusing or that are important to answering the question.

✓ **Double-check** to make sure you have answered everything before handing in your test.

When taking tests, some words are often overlooked. Failure to pay close attention to these words can result in an incorrect answer. One way to avoid this is to be aware of these words and to <u>underline,</u> circle or highlight these words while you are taking the test.

Even though these words are easy, they can change the meaning of the entire question and/or answer.

all	always	most likely	probably	best	not
difference	usually	except	most	unlikely	likely

Example

1. During the race, Susan is **most likely** feeling

   A. sad
   B. weak
   C. scared
   D. determined

HELPFUL STRATEGIES FOR ANSWERING MULTIPLE-CHOICE QUESTIONS

A multiple-choice question provides some information for you to consider and then asks you to select a response from four choices. There will be one correct answer. The other answers are distractors, which are incorrect.

Here are some strategies to help you when answering multiple-choice questions.

- ✓ Quickly skim through the entire test. Find out how many questions there are and plan your time accordingly.

- ✓ Read and reread questions carefully. Underline key words and try to think of an answer before looking at the choices.

- ✓ If there is a graphic, look at the graphic, read the question, and go back to the graphic. Then, you may want to circle the important information from the question.

- ✓ Carefully read the choices. Read the question first and then each answer with it.

✓ When choosing an answer, try to eliminate those choices that are clearly wrong or do not make sense.

✓ Some questions may ask you to select the "best" answer. These questions will always include words like **best**, **most strongly**, and **most clearly**. All of the answers will be correct to some degree, but one of the choices will be "best" in some way. Carefully read all four choices (A, B, C, D) before choosing the answer you think is the best.

✓ If you do not know the answer or if the question does not make sense to you, it is better to guess than to leave it blank.

✓ Do not spend too much time on any one question. Make a mark (*) beside a difficult question and come back to it. If you are leaving a question to come back to later, make sure that you also leave the space on the answer sheet.

✓ Remember to go back to the difficult questions at the end of the test; sometimes clues are given throughout the test that will provide you with answers.

✓ Note any negative (e.g., **no**, **not**) and be sure your choice fits the question.

✓ Before changing an answer, **be sure** you have a very good reason to do so.

✓ Do not look for patterns on your answer sheet.

HELPFUL STRATEGIES FOR ANSWERING WRITTEN-RESPONSE QUESTIONS

A written response requires you to respond to a question or directive such as explain, predict, list, describe, use information from the text and your own ideas; provide the main idea and supporting details. In preparing for open-response tasks you may wish to:

✓ Read and re-read the question carefully.

✓ Recognize and pay close attention to directing words such as explain, predict, and describe.

✓ <u>Underline</u> key words and phrases that indicate what is required in your answer such as <u>explain</u>, <u>summarize,</u> <u>mainly about</u>, <u>what is the meaning of,</u> <u>best shows…</u>

✓ Write down rough, point-form notes regarding the information you want to include in your answer.

✓ Think about what you want to say and organize information and ideas in a coherent and concise manner within the time limit you have for the question.

✓ Be sure to answer every part of the question that is asked.

✓ Stick to the question, be brief and only answer what is asked.

✓ Answer in full and correctly written sentences keeping your answer within the space provided.

✓ Re-read your response to ensure you have answered the question.

✓ **Think!** Does your answer make sense

✓ **Listen!** Does it sound right?

✓ Use the appropriate subject vocabulary and terminology in your response.

SUMMARY OF HOW TO BE SUCCESSFUL DURING THE TEST

✓ The following are some strategies that you may find useful in writing your test.

✓ Take 2 or 3 deep breaths to help you relax.

✓ Read the directions carefully and underline, circle, or highlight any *KEY* words.

✓ Survey the entire test to get a flavour of what you will need to do.

✓ Budget your time.

✓ Begin with an easy question or a question that you know that you can answer correctly rather than following the numerical question order of the test.

✓ If you "draw a blank" on the test, try repeating the deep breathing and physical relaxation activities first. Then, move to visualization and positive self-talk to get you going.

✓ Write down anything that you remember about the subject on the reverse side of your test paper. This activity sometimes helps you to remind yourself that you do know something and you are capable of writing the test.

✓ Look over your test when you have finished and double-check your answers to be sure you did not forget anything.

NOTES

120

Part A: A Guide to Writing the Provincial Achievement Test

TABLE OF CORRELATIONS			
General Outcome	**Specific Outcome**	**Practice Questions**	**Unit Test**
Students are expected to …			
2.1 Use strategies and cues	2.1.3.2 attend to and use knowledge of capitalization, commas in a series, question marks, exclamation marks and quotation marks to read accurately, fluently and with comprehension during oral and silent reading	Writing Prompt	Writing Prompt
2.4 Create original text	2.4.1.1 experiment with ways of generating and organizing ideas prior to creating oral, print and other media texts	Writing Prompt	Writing Prompt
	2.4.2.1 use sentence variety to link ideas and create impressions on familiar audiences	Writing Prompt	Writing Prompt
	2.4.3.1 experiment with a variety of story beginnings to choose ones that best introduce particular stories	Writing Prompt	Writing Prompt
	2.4.3.2 add sufficient detail to oral, print and other media texts to tell about setting and character, and to sustain plot	Writing Prompt	Writing Prompt
3.3 Organize, record and evaluate	3.3.1.1 organize ideas using a variety of strategies, such as clustering, categorizing and sequencing	Writing Prompt	Writing Prompt
	3.3.1.2 draft ideas and information into short paragraphs, with topic and supporting sentences	Writing Prompt	Writing Prompt
4.1 Enhance and improve	4.1.2.2 edit for complete and incomplete sentences	Writing Prompt	Writing Prompt
	4.1.5.1 choose words, language patterns, illustrations or sounds to add detail and create desired effects in oral, print and other media texts	Writing Prompt	Writing Prompt

4.2 Attend to conventions	4.2.1.1 identify a variety of sentence types, and use in own writing	Writing Prompt	Writing Prompt
	4.2.1.2 identify correct subject-verb agreement, and use in own writing	Writing Prompt	Writing Prompt
	4.2.1.3 use adjectives and adverbs to add interest and detail to own writing	Writing Prompt	Writing Prompt
	4.2.1.4 distinguish between complete and incomplete sentences	Writing Prompt	Writing Prompt
	4.2.2.1 use phonic knowledge and skills and visual memory, systematically, to spell phonically regular, three-syllable words in own writing	Writing Prompt	Writing Prompt
	4.2.2.2 identify generalizations that assist with the spelling of unfamiliar words, including irregular plurals in own writing	Writing Prompt	Writing Prompt
	4.2.2.3 identify frequently misspelled words, and develop strategies for learning to spell them correctly in own writing	Writing Prompt	Writing Prompt
	4.2.3.2 use exclamation marks, appropriately, as end punctuation in own writing	Writing Prompt	Writing Prompt
	4.2.3.3 use apostrophes to form common contractions and to show possession in own writing	Writing Prompt	Writing Prompt
	4.2.3.4 identify commas, end punctuation, apostrophes and quotation marks when reading, and use them to assist comprehension	Writing Prompt	Writing Prompt
4.3 Present and Share	4.3.1.1 present ideas and information on a topic, using a pre-established plan	Writing Prompt	Writing Prompt

PART A: A GUIDE TO WRITING THE PROVINCIAL ACHIEVEMENT TEST (PAT)

For Part A of the PAT, you will be given a picture prompt to help you decide on what you will write about. Your writing will be a story that is real or imagined and should be based on what you see in the picture you are given. Your story should show your understanding of creating interesting content using main ideas and details; following good organization with an introduction, actions and events, and a conclusion; controlled sentence structure; appropriate use of vocabulary; and Grade 3 level uses of conventions. Your story will be rated as meeting the standard of excellence, approaching the standard of excellence, clearly meeting the acceptable standard, not clearly meeting the acceptable standard, or clearly below the acceptable standard.

Your writing will be marked using the following scoring rubric:

SCORING RUBRIC

CONTENT

Focus

When marking **CONTENT** appropriate for Grade 3 writing, the marker should consider how effectively the writer

- establishes the relationship between events, actions, and context (situation)
- uses specific details
- demonstrates the reader/writer relationship (voice)

Meets the Standard of Excellence

Excellent E	• Events, actions, and/or ideas are creative and are consistent with the context established by the writer. • Details are precise and consistently effective. • The writing is confident, holds the reader's interest, and presentsa well-supported main idea.

Approaches the Standard of Excellence

Proficient Pf	• Events, actions, and/or ideas are intentionally chosen and are appropriate for the context established by the writer. • Details are specific and generally effective. • The writing is purposeful, draws the reader's interest, and presents a supported main idea.

Clearly Meets the Acceptable Standard

Satisfactory S	• Events, actions, and/or ideas are generally appropriate for the context established by the writer. • Details are general and may be predictable, but are appropriate. • The writing is straightforward and generally holds the reader's interest and provides some support for a main idea.

Does Not Clearly Meet the Acceptable Standard

Limited L	• Events, actions, and/or ideas are vague and may not be appropriate for the context established by the writer. • Details are few and/or may be repetitive. • The writing is ambiguous, it does not hold the reader's interest, and the main idea is superficial.

Clearly Below the Acceptable Standard

Poor P	• Events, actions, and/or ideas are undeveloped and/or inappropriate. • Details are scant. • The writing is confusing and/or frustrating for the reader, and a main idea is lacking.

Insufficient

Insufficient INS	• The marker can discern no evidence of an attempt to fulfill the assignment, or the writing is so deficient in length that it is not possible to assess Content. • *Note:* **Content** *and* **Organization** *are weighted to be worth twice as much as each of the other categories.*

ORGANIZATION

Focus

When marking **ORGANIZATION** appropriate for Grade 3 writing, the marker should consider how effectively the writer

- introduces the response
- establishes the connections and/or relationships between events, actions, details, and/or characters
- brings closure to the writing

Meets the Standard of Excellence

Excellent E	• The beginning is purposeful and effectively establishes events, characters, and/or setting and provides direction for the writing. • Connections and/or relationships between events, actions, details, and/or characters are developed and consistently maintained. • The ending effectively ties events and/or actions together.

Approaches the Standard of Excellence

Proficient Pf	• The beginning clearly establishes events, characters, and/or setting and provides direction for the writing. • Connections and/or relationships between events, actions, details, and/or characters are maintained. • The ending clearly provides an appropriate finish for events and/or actions.

Clearly Meets the Acceptable Standard

Satisfactory S	• The beginning directly presents information about events, characters, and/or setting. • Connections and/or relationships between events, actions, details, and/or characters are generally maintained. • The ending is predictable and/or may be contrived but is connected to events and/or actions.

Does Not Clearly Meet the Acceptable Standard

Limited L	• The beginning presents information about events, characters, and/or setting but lacks direction. • Connections and/or relationships between events, actions, details, and/or characters are unclear or inconsistent. • The ending is predictable and/or contrived.

Clearly Below the Acceptable Standard

Poor P	• The beginning provides little information and/or is ineffective. • Connections and/or relationships between events, actions, details, and/or characters are missing. • The ending, if present, is unconnected to the events and/or actions

Insufficient

INS	• The writing has been awarded an INS for Content. • *Note:* **Content** *and* **Organization** *are weighted to be worth twice as much as each of the other categories.*

SENTENCE STRUCTURE

Focus

When marking **SENTENCE STRUCTURE** appropriate for Grade 3 writing, the marker should consider how effectively the writer

- controls sentence structure
- uses different sentence patterns and length
- uses a variety of sentence beginnings

The length and complexity of response must be considered.

Meets the Standard of Excellence

| Excellent

E	• Sentence structure is consistently controlled. • Sentence type and length are varied and effective. • Sentence beginnings are consistently varied.

Approaches the Standard of Excellence

| Proficient

Pf	• Sentence structure is controlled. • Sentence type and length are usually varied and effective. • Sentence beginnings are often varied.

Clearly Meets the Acceptable Standard

| Satisfactory

S	• Sentence structure is generally controlled but may occasionally impede the meaning. • Sentences may vary in type and length. • Some variety of sentence beginnings is evident.

Does Not Clearly Meet the Acceptable Standard

Limited L	• Sentence structure is sometimes lacking control, and this often impedes meaning. • There is little variation of sentence type and/or length. • There is little variety of sentence beginnings.

Clearly Below the Acceptable Standard

Poor P	• Thought units are difficult to recognize, and this severely impedes the meaning. • There is no variation of sentence type and/or length. • There is no variety of sentence beginnings.

Insufficient

INS	• The writing has been awarded an INS for Content.

VOCABULARY

Focus

When marking **VOCABULARY** appropriate for Grade 3 writing, the marker should consider the extent to which the writer uses

- words appropriately
- expressions effectively
- words and expressions to enhance the writing

The length and complexity of response must be considered.

MEETS THE STANDARD OF EXCELLENCE

Excellent E	• Well-chosen words are used effectively. • Expressions are consistently precise and effective. • Words and expressions are used to create vivid images and enhance the writing.

Approaches the Standard of Excellence

Proficient P	• Well-chosen words are often used. • Expressions are usually specific and effective. • Words and expressions are descriptive and often enhance the writing.

Clearly Meets the Acceptable Standard

Satisfactory S	• Words chosen tend to be common or ordinary. • Expressions are usually more general than specific. • Words and expressions sometimes enhance the writing.

Does Not Clearly Meet the Acceptable Standard

| Limited

L	• Words used indicate a lack of vocabulary. • Expressions are simplistic and/or ineffective. • Words and expressions are basic and may detract from the writing..

Clearly Below the Acceptable Standard

| Poor

P	• Words chosen are sometimes inappropriate or misused. • Expressions are misused or missing. • Words and expressions are inadequate.

Insufficient

INS	• The writing has been awarded an INS for Content.

CONVENTIONS

FOCUS

When marking **CONVENTIONS** appropriate for Grade 3 writing, the marker should consider the extent to which the writer has control of

- end punctuation and capitalization
- spelling
- usage and clarity through grammar

Proportion of error to length and complexity of response must be considered.

Meets the Standard of Excellence

Excellent E	<ul><li>End punctuation and capitalization are correct.</li><li>Most words, familiar and unfamiliar, are spelled correctly; spelling errors are understandable "slips."</li><li>Errors that are present do not affect the clarity or effectiveness of communication.</li></ul>

Approaches the Standard of Excellence

Proficient P	<ul><li>End punctuation and capitalization are essentially correct.</li><li>Familiar words are spelled correctly; spelling errors are "slips"; unfamiliar words may be spelled phonetically.</li><li>Errors that are present rarely affect the clarity of communication.</li></ul>

Clearly Meets the Acceptable Standard

Satisfactory S	<ul><li>Conventional end punctuation and capitalization are usually correct.</li><li>Many familiar words are spelled correctly; errors suggest uneven control of spelling rules; unfamiliar words are generally spelled phonetically.</li><li>Errors are sometimes intrusive and may affect the clarity of communication.</li></ul>

Does Not Clearly Meet the Acceptable Standard

Limited L	• End punctuation and capitalization, when present, are inconsistent. • Many familiar words are misspelled and/or spelled phonetically. • Errors interfere with the clarity of communication.

Clearly Below the Acceptable Standard

Poor P	• There is little, if any, evidence that the writer understands correct use of end punctuation and capitalization. • Words may be difficult to discern and are generally spelled phonetically. • Communication is not clear.

Insufficient

INS	• There is little, if any, evidence that the writer understands correct use of end punctuation and capitalization. • Words may be difficult to discern and are generally spelled phonetically. • Communication is not clear.

The next section of your KEY gives you some help in improving your writing to make sure that you receive a rank of meeting the acceptable standard (S) and hopefully improve your writing even more to earn a score of Pf or E.

In this section, you will be given practice questions that look like the Provincial Achievement Test and you will also receive sample responses for each picture prompt. The first sample will be rated as an S response and then you will be given a sample Pf and E response to show you how to improve an S score and take it to a Pf or E score.

PRACTICE QUESTIONS—WRITING

NARRATIVE WRITING—1

DESCRIPTION

For this test, you have 10 minutes for discussion, 10 minutes for planning, and 50 minutes to complete your writing. You may take up to 30 extra minutes to complete the test, if you need it.

INSTRUCTIONS

- Read the story starter as your teacher reads it aloud.

- Talk with your classmates about the writing activity or think about it by yourself.

- Plan your writing in whatever way you choose (web, list, pictures, etc.).

- Choose the kind of writing (story, letter, diary/journal entries) that will allow you to show your **best** writing.

- When you are doing your writing, print or write as neatly as you can.

- When you have finished, **check your work carefully** and correct any mistakes.

Look at the picture carefully. What do you think is about to happen? Write an exciting story about what happens.

_____

_____

_____

_____

_____

_____

_____

_____

_____

_____

_____

_____

_____

_____

_____

_____

_____

_____

_____

_____

_____

_____

_____

_____

_____

_____

_____

_____

_____

_____

_____

NARRATIVE WRITING—2

DESCRIPTION

For this test, you have 10 minutes for discussion, 10 minutes for planning, and 50 minutes to complete your writing. You may take up to 30 extra minutes to complete the test, if you need it.

INSTRUCTIONS

- Read the story starter as your teacher reads it aloud.

- Talk with your classmates about the writing activity or think about it by yourself.

- Plan your writing in whatever way you choose (web, list, pictures, etc.).

- Choose the kind of writing (story, letter, diary/journal entries) that will allow you to show your **best** writing.

- When you are doing your writing, print or write as neatly as you can.

- When you have finished, **check your work carefully** and correct any mistakes.

Look carefully at the picture. What do you think is happening? What do you think will happen next? Write an exciting story about what happens.

_____

_____

_____

_____

_____

_____

_____

_____

_____

_____

_____

_____

_____

_____

_____

_____

_____

_____

_____

_____

_____

_____

_____

_____

_____

_____

_____

_____

_____

_____

_____

_____

NARRATIVE WRITING—3

DESCRIPTION

For this test, you have 10 minutes for discussion, 10 minutes for planning, and 50 minutes to complete your writing. You may take up to 30 extra minutes to complete the test, if you need it.

INSTRUCTIONS

- Read the story starter as your teacher reads it aloud.

- Talk with your classmates about the writing activity or think about it by yourself.

- Plan your writing in whatever way you choose (web, list, pictures, etc.).

- Choose the kind of writing (story, letter, diary/journal entries) that will allow you to show your **best** writing.

- When you are doing your writing, print or write as neatly as you can.

- When you have finished, **check your work carefully** and correct any mistakes.

Look carefully at the picture. What do you think is happening? What do you think will happen next? Write an exciting story about what happens.

_____
_____
_____
_____
_____
_____
_____
_____
_____
_____
_____
_____
_____
_____
_____
_____
_____
_____
_____
_____
_____
_____
_____
_____
_____
_____
_____
_____
_____
_____

SAMPLE RESPONSES TO PRACTICE QUESTIONS

SCORE S RESPONSE

One day me and my brothers went camping. When my mom and dad had gone for a walk we stayed by the camp fire, we did'nt see the alians coming out of there space ship to us. Then we saw them and I said WOW look at those creters and Tyler said they are alians from out of space. They walked across the river and came to us and said we want to be your friend because we have just landed on earth and we are hungary. Tyler went into the tent and came out with some hot dogs and we poked them with sticks and put them in the fire and cooked them and then we gave them to the alians to eat. They really liked them! And they eat 4 each. Then the alians told us about there plannet and it was awsome because everything on it is green. It is called the green plannet. Then the alians said they had to go and thanked us and walked back to there space ship and it just vanished. When mom and dad came back we told them about the alians and they said how exiting and we all went to bed.

RATIONALE FOR GRADE 3 NARRATIVE WRITING MARK S

Score		Reporting Category
S		**Content:**
	S	**The events, actions, and ideas are generally appropriate for the context established by the writer** (three children are camping when they see aliens approach them from their spaceship).
	S	**Details are general, but are appropriate for the story,** such as "They walked across the river and came to us," "we have just landed on earth and we are hungry," and "alians told us about there plannet."
	S	**The writing is straightforward, generally holds the reader's interest, and provides some support for a main idea** as it tells about the children meeting and communicating with the aliens.

S		**Organization:**
	S	**The beginning directly presents information about events,** such as "One day me and my brothers went camping," characters, such as "me and my brothers," and setting, such as "we stayed by the camp fire."
	S	**Connections and/or relationships between events, actions, details, and/or characters are generally maintained,** such as "said we want to be your friend because we have just landed on earth" and "the alians said they had to go and thanked us."
	S	**The ending,** "When mom and dad came back we told them about the alians and they said how exiting and we all went to bed," **is predictable and contrived but is connected to events and actions.**
S		**Sentence Structure:**
	S	**Sentence structure is generally controlled, but run-on sentences are present,** such as "we stayed by the camp fire, we di'dnt see the alians coming" and "they said how exiting and we all went to bed." **These may occasionally impede the meaning.**
	S	**Sentences may vary in type and length,** such as "Then the alians told us about there planet and it was awsome because everything on it is green" and "It is called the green planet."
	S	**Some variety of sentence beginnings,** such as "One day," "When my mom," and "Tyler went," **is evident.**
		The length and complexity of the response has been considered.

S	S	**Vocabulary:** **Words chosen,** such as "mom and dad had gone for a walk" and "Then we saw them," **tend to be common or ordinary.**
	S	**Expressions,** such as "they are alians from out of space" and "we poked them with sticks and put them in the fire and cooked them," **are usually more general than specific.**
	S	**Words and expressions,** such as "WOW" and "it was awesome," **sometimes enhance the writing.** **The length and complexity of the response has been considered.**
S		**Conventions:**
	S	**Conventional end punctuation and capitalization are usually correct.**
	S	**Many familiar words,** such as "camping," "friend," and "vanished" **are spelled correctly; errors,** such as "did'nt," "creters," "hungary," and "there," **suggest uneven control of spelling rules; unfamiliar words,** such as "alians" and "planet," **are generally spelled phonetically.**
	S	**Errors,** such as "how exiting," **are sometimes intrusive and may affect the clarity of communication.** **The length and complexity of the response has been considered.**

SCORE PF RESPONSE

> The Aliens
>
> I felt very excited because we were going camping for the first time this summer. We all got ready and packed the tents and things and then we drove to our very favourite place. It was in the woods and a rushing river was near by and we could catch fish and swim in the river. After setting up the tent and putting our sleeping bags inside and having a apple mom and dad lighted the fire and then went to find more wood so we could cook hot dogs and roast marshmellows for supper. Tracy and me were just sitting there by the fire when we saw a bright shiny light across the river. The light turned into a space ship and it landed and out of it came three little green aliens with big round heads and antenas sticking out of the top of their heads. "Look at that!" I yelled at Tracy. "WOW!!" she said. "What do they want? I wondered. They walked across the river and did'nt seem to notice that it was very cold and they came towards us. We were very frightend but they were nice and one of them beamed us a message that said we just landed on this planet and we are lost and hungry. Do you know where we are? I said "You are on earth and we can give you some apples and hot dogs if you like." They said "Yes please and if we are on earth we know how to get back to our planet by flying though the milky way." After they had eaten their food they thanked us and went back to their space ship and we watched them take off with a WOOSH and then they dissapeared into the darkness.

RATIONALE FOR GRADE 3 NARRATIVE WRITING MARK PF

Score		Reporting Category
Pf		**Content:**
	Pf	**Events, actions, and ideas are appropriate for the context established by the writer** (children are camping when they see a space ship and aliens land on the other side of the river).
	Pf	**Details,** such as "we could catch fish and swim in the river," "we saw a bright shiny light," and "The light turned into a space ship," **are specific and generally effective.**
	Pf	**The writing draws the reader's interest and presents a supported main idea:** "We just landed on this planet."

Pf	**Pf**	**Organization:** **The beginning,** "I felt very excited because we were going camping for the first time this summer. We all got ready and packed the tents and things and then we drove to our very favourite place. It was in the woods and a rushing river was near by and we could catch fish and swim in the river," **clearly establishes events, characters, and setting and provides direction for the writing.**
	Pf	**Connections and/or relationships between events, actions, details, and characters are maintained,** such as "mom and dad lighted the fire and then went to find more wood," "out of it came three little green aliens," and "We were very frightend."
	Pf	**The ending,** "After they had eaten their food they thanked us and went back to their space ship and we watched them take off with a WOOSH and then they dissappeared into the darkness," **provides an appropriate finish for events and actions.**
Pf	**Pf**	**Sentence Structure:** **Sentence structure is controlled:** "Tracy and me were just sitting there by the fire when we saw a bright shiny light across the river."
	Pf	**Sentence type and sentence length,** such as "What do they want?" and "We were very frightend but they were nice and one of them beamed us a message that said we just landed on this planet and we are lost and hungry," **are usually varied and effective.**
	Pf	**Sentence beginnings,** such as "After setting up," "The light turned," and "Do you know," **are often varied.** **The length and complexity of the response has been considered.**

Pf		
		Vocabulary:
	Pf	**Well-chosen words,** such as "rushing river" and "a bright shiny light," **are often used.**
	Pf	**Expressions,** such as "three little green aliens with big round heads and antenas sticking out of the top of their heads" and "beamed us a message," **are usually specific and effective.**
	Pf	**Words and expressions, such as** "'WOW!!'" "'get back to our planet by flying though the milky way,'" and "WOOSH," **are descriptive and often enhance the writing.**
		The length and complexity of the response has been considered.
Pf		**Conventions:**
	Pf	**End punctuation and capitalization are essentially correct.**
	Pf	**Familiar words are spelled correctly; spelling errors,** such as "frightend" and "dissappeared," **are "slips"; unfamiliar words,** such as "marshmellows" and "antenas," **may be spelled phonetically.**
	Pf	**Errors that are present,** such as "Tracy and me," "did'nt seem," and "the milky way" **rarely affect the clarity of communication.**
		The length and complexity of the response has been considered.

SCORE E RESPONSE

What a Camping Trip!

"Now remember to stay close to the camp sight and don't let the fire go out" said Dad when he and Mom set off for their usual night time walk. My brothers and me were used to this, every night after supper Mom and Dad went for a walk and left us to look after our things. Tonight was different. There was a bright full moon in the sky and the stars were extra bright and sparkling. Suddenly what looked like a falling star came crashing down to earth just across the river. "Wow! Awesome!" we cried out in amazement. We realized it was not a falling star because it was shaped like a space ship and climbing slowly down a ladder came three crimson red aliens. They had large heads with one big bulgeing eye, two legs that were so long they looked like spiders and two arms that had eight fingers on each hand. They skipped towards the bubbling river and noisily splashed across the cold water. When they reached our camp sight they beamed a message to us through their big eye and said "We are friendly aliens and we wonder if you would like to come for a ride in our space ship." "YES! YES!" we shouted together. "This is so exciting and amazing." "But…but…but what about Mom and Dad?" asked my little brother. "Don't worry." said one of the aliens. "We will have you back before your parents return."

We rushed as fast as a speeding bullet to get our shoes and jackets and then we went with the aliens across the river to their space ship. I had to help Bobby up the ladder because he couldn't reach the steps but we made it and once the door was shut we blasted off. We felt like we were on a speed boat but suddenly everything became smooth and we glided over the earth. We looked out the window and saw the rocky mountains and lakes and then we were over the ocean and could see dolphins and hump back whales swimming in the sea. We climbed higher and higher until the earth was a big round blue globe below us. It was truly miraculous and just like the pictures that I had seen in books. All too quickly we were back on earth beside the gurgling river and across from our camp sight. We thanked the aliens for an awesome adventure and said we would never forget them and we would tell everyone that aliens are really friendly and nice. They said "See you next year and we will take you for another ride into space!" We got back to the camp before Mom and Dad and decided to keep our visit with the aliens a secret.

RATIONALE FOR GRADE 3 NARRATIVE WRITING MARK E

Score		Reporting Category
E		**Content:**
	E	**Events, actions, and ideas are creative and consistent with the context established by the writer** (three children see a space ship with aliens, descend to Earth, and they travel with the aliens for a visit to outer space).
	E	**Details,** such as "came crashing down to earth just across the river" and "they beamed a message to us through their big eye," **are precise and consistently effective,** and the reader experiences the writer's excitement with the arrival of the aliens.
	E	**The writing is confident, holds the reader's interest, and presents a well-supported main idea:** "'We are friendly aliens and we wonder if you would like to come for a ride in our space ship.'"
E		**Organization:**
	E	**The beginning,** "'Now remember to stay close to the camp sight and don't let the fire go out'" said Dad when he and Mom set off for their usual night time walk. My brothers and me were used to this, every night after supper Mom and Dad went for a walk and left us to look after our things," **is purposeful and effectively establishes events, characters, and setting and provides direction for the writing.**
	E	**Connections and/or relationships between events, actions, details, and characters are developed and consistently maintained,** such as "it was shaped like a space ship and climbing slowly down a ladder came three crimson red aliens," "we were over the ocean and could see dolphins and hump back whales swimming," and "We climbed higher and higher until the earth was a big round blue globe below us."
	E	**The ending,** "We thanked the aliens for an awesome adventure and said we would never forget them and we would tell everyone that aliens are really friendly and nice. They said 'See you next year and we will take you for another ride into space!' We got back to the camp before Mom and Dad and decided to keep our visit with the aliens a secret," **effectively ties events and actions together.**

E	**E**	**Sentence Structure:**
		Sentence structure is consistently controlled, such as "'But… but…but what about Mom and Dad?'"
	E	**Sentence type and sentence length,** such as "Tonight was different" and "I had to help Bobby up the ladder because he couldn't reach the steps but we made it and once the door was shut we blasted off," **are varied and effective.**
	E	**Sentence beginnings,** such as "Now remember," "Suddenly what looked," "We rushed," and "All too quickly," **are consistently varied.**
		The length and complexity of the response has been considered.
E	**E**	**Vocabulary:**
		Well-chosen words, such as "bright full moon in the sky and the stars were extra bright and sparkling" and "skipped towards the bubbling river and noisily splashed across," **are used effectively.**
	E	**Expressions,** such as "came crashing down," "'Wow! Awesome!'" "'YES! YES!'" and "was truly miraculous," **are consistently precise and effective.**
	E	**Words and expressions,** such as "three crimson red aliens," "large heads with one big bulgeing eye, two legs that were so long they looked like spiders and two arms that had eight fingers on each hand," "as fast as a speeding bullet," and "the gurgling river," **are used to create vivid images and enhance the writing.**
		The length and complexity of the response has been considered.

E		**Conventions:**
	E	**End punctuation and capitalization are correct.**
	E	**Most words, familiar and unfamiliar, are spelled correctly;** **spelling errors such as** "camp sight" and "bulgeing" **are** **understandable "slips."**
	E	**Errors that are present,** such as "My brothers and me" and "rocky mountains," **do not affect the clarity or effectiveness of communication.**
		The length and complexity of the response has been considered.

RESPONSES TO NARRATIVE WRITING PROMPT 2
SCORE S RESPONSE

The Balloon man

"hey Taylor wanna go to my house"

"Sure" said Taylor, wait a sec… What's all that screaming"

"Lets go see" said David. They went to were the screaming was and saw a Nesreporter say "he's done it. Ladies and gentalman. Bobby has done it." "Done wat" said Taylor and David.

"He's flying of in balloons and he's also making a world record!" said the news reporter. "But wait how will he get down." said David. "He has sizers" said the news reporter.

"No he dosen't, they're right there!" said Taylor. "Oh no. How will we get him down." said the news reporter. "Lets throw them up to him" said David. "OK" said the news reporter.

Then they tried to throw Bobby the sizers but they couldn't throw that high. "Lets find a seagull to fly the sizers to him" said David. They found a seagull and tyed the sizers to his legs and threw him up to the balloons. Then Bobby cought them and cut the balloon string, and then Bobby fell and broke his foot…

Then he went to the hospital and got cured and never went back to his job.

RATIONALE FOR GRADE 3 NARRATIVE WRITING MARK S

Score		Reporting Category
S		**Content:**
	S	**The majority of the events, actions, and ideas are generally appropriate for the context established by the writer** (two children see a balloon man being lifted into the air by his balloons).
	S	**Details are general, but are appropriate for the story,** such as "'He's flying of in balloons'" and "'He has sizers.'"
	S	**The writing is straightforward and generally holds the reader's interest and provides some support for a main idea** as it tells about the balloon man trying to make a world record and the crowd's concern about how he will get down.
S		**Organization:**
	S	**The beginning directly presents information about events, characters, and setting,** such as "They went to were the screaming was and saw a Nesreporter say 'he's done it, ladies and gentalman. Bobby has done it.' 'Done wat' said Taylor and David. 'He's flying of in balloons and he's also making a world record!'"
	S	**Connections and/or relationships between events, actions, details, and/or characters are generally maintained,** such as "They went to were the screaming was" and "Bobby cought them and cut the balloon string."
	S	**The ending,** "Bobby fell and broke his foot…Then he went to the hospital and got cured and never went back to his job," **is predictable and contrived, but is connected to events and actions.**

S	S	**Sentence Structure:**
		Sentence structure is generally controlled but sentence fragments are present, such as "'Ladies and gentalman.'", **may occasionally impede the meaning.**
	S	**Sentences may vary in type and length,** such as "'Lets go see' said David" and "Then they tried to throw Bobby the sizers but they couldn't throw that high."
	S	**Some variety of sentence beginnings,** such as "hey Taylor," "What's all," and "They found," **is evident.**
		The length and complexity of the response has been considered.
S		**Vocabulary:**
	S	**Words chosen,** such as "go see" and "they couldn't throw that high," **tend to be common or ordinary.**
	S	**Expressions,** such as "wanna go to my house" and "found a seagull and tyed the sizers to his legs," **are usually more general than specific.**
	S	**Words and expressions,** such as "he's done it" and "world record," **sometimes enhance the writing.**
		The length and complexity of the response has been considered.
S		**Conventions:**
	S	**Conventional end punctuation and capitalization are usually correct.**
	S	**Many familiar words,** such as "screaming," "Ladies," and "hospital," **are spelled correctly; errors,** such as "Lets," "gentalman," "dosen't," "tyed," and "cought," **suggest uneven control of spelling rules; unfamiliar words** such as "wanna" and "sizers" **are generally spelled phonetically.**
	S	**Errors,** such as "went to were" and "Nesreporter," **are sometimes intrusive and may affect the clarity of communication.**
		The length and complexity of the response has been considered.

SCORE PF RESPONSE

Trouble at the Carnival

One fine sunny day Billy and Sally's mom and dad said that they were going to take them to the carnival. Billy and Sally screamed with excitement "whoooohooo" and then they raced to get ready. When they got to the carnival they saw all sorts of things to see. There were rides and games and clowns and a balloon man selling his brightly coloured humungus balloons. First they all got some cotton candy and hot dog and then they went into the haunted house. There were ghosts hovering in walls and big black bats flying around scaring the people but Billy and Sally were not really scared. After that they decided to go on the ferris wheel. Billy and Sally waited in line and when they got on they sat together. The ride was climbing up into the sky when sudenly it stopped and they were stuck right at the top of the ferris wheel. They looked up and they were so surprised when they saw the balloon man floating into the air passed them. They called out to him but he could'nt hear them because of all the noise and the birds flying by. As soon as the ride was fixed and they got down Billy and Sally raced to the helicopter ride and climbed into a blue one. As the helicopter took off it turned into a real one and they flew it up to the balloon man. "Do you want a rescue"? asked Billy. "Sure" said the balloon man. So the children helped him climb into the helicopter. But first he had to cut the balloons from his rist and they watched them float gently away making the sky look yellow and green and red and blue. Then they flew the helicopter back to its ride and parked it carefully on the ride and they all celebrated by having a ice cream and a slurpee because they were so tired and hot after the rescue.

RATIONALE FOR GRADE 3 NARRATIVE WRITING MARK Pf

Score		Reporting Category
Pf	Pf	**Content:** **Events, actions, and ideas are appropriate for the context established by the writer** (two children go to the carnival and see a balloon man being carried away by his balloons).
	Pf	**Details,** such as "they went into the haunted house," "they saw the balloon man floating into the air passed them," and "they flew it up to the balloon man," **are specific and generally effective.**
	Pf	**The writing engages the reader's interest and presents a supported main idea:** "a balloon man selling his brightly coloured humungus balloons."
Pf	Pf	**Organization:** **The beginning,** "One fine sunny day Billy and Sally's mom and dad said that they were going to take them to the carnival. Billy and Sally screamed with excitement "whoooohooo" and then they raced to get ready. When they got to the carnival they saw all sorts of things to see. There were rides and games and clowns and a balloon man selling his brightly coloured humungus balloons," **clearly establishes events, characters, and setting and provides direction for the writing.**
	Pf	**Connections and/or relationships between events, actions, details, and characters are maintained,** such as "they decided to go on the ferris wheel," "he could'nt hear them because of all the noise," and "he had to cut the balloons from his rist."
	Pf	**The ending,** "the children helped him climb into the helicopter. But first he had to cut the balloons from his rist and they watched them float gently away making the sky look yellow and green and red and blue. Then they flew the helicopter back to its ride and parked it carefully on the ride and they all celebrated by having a ice cream and a slurpee because they were so tired and hot after the rescue," **provides an appropriate finish for events and actions.**

Pf		**Sentence Structure:**
	Pf	**Sentence structure is controlled,** such as "First they all got some cotton candy and hot dog and then they went into the haunted house."
	Pf	**Sentence type and sentence length,** such as "The ride was climbing up into the sky when sudenly it stopped and they were stuck right at the top of the ferris wheel" and "'Do you want a rescue?'" **are usually varied and effective.**
	Pf	**Sentence beginnings,** such as "One fine sunny day," "After that they," and "As the helicopter took off," **are often varied.**
		The length and complexity of the response has been considered.
Pf		**Vocabulary:**
	Pf	**Well-chosen words,** such as "big black bats flying around," "climbing up into the sky," and "celebrated," **are often used.**
	Pf	**Expressions,** such as "brightly coloured humungus balloons" and "float gently away making the sky look yellow and green and red and blue," **are usually specific and effective.**
	Pf	**Words and expressions,** such as "screamed with excitement 'whoooohooo,'" "ghosts hovering in walls," and "the balloon man floating into the air," **are descriptive and often enhance the writing.**
		The length and complexity of the response has been considered.
Pf		**Conventions:**
	Pf	**End punctuation and capitalization are essentially correct.**
	Pf	**Familiar words are spelled correctly; spelling errors,** such as "sudenly" and "could'nt," are "slips"; unfamiliar words, such as "humungus" and "rist," **may be spelled phonetically.**
	Pf	**Errors that are present,** such as "candy and hot dog" and "floating into the air passed," **rarely affect the clarity of communication.**
		The length and complexity of the response has been considered.

SCORE E RESPONSE

> ### Bobo the clown
>
> "Look" screamed Luke to Kayla his best friend.
>
> "What? Wow" cried Kayla. "Look at all of the balloons and it looks like there's a clown hanging down from them." "Yeah your right" yelled Luke "let's try and rescue him and get him down." "Okay" said Kayla. "Hey look over there at the gum ball machine. Let's get some gum." They raced to the machine and got some huba baba gum. They blew the biggest bubbles ever and they started to lift up into the sky. As Kayla got over the beach she was so close to grabbing hold of the clown's big foot when her huba baba gum popped and Kayla yelled "Ahhhhhhhhh!" She was just about to fall into the ocean when Luke grabbed her hand and said "Be careful". They were too heavy for Luke's huba baba gum so they landed on the beach with a bump. Luckily they were not hurt. After a while they decided to get a hot air balloon. After climbing into the basket they took off and the wind flew them towards the beach. They searched and searched the sky for the clown and a few hours later they saw him in the distance. He looked like a kite flying in the sky with balloons pulling him along. Luke and Kayla almost fell out of the basket as they helped the clown climb into it. The clown said "Thank you, and by the way my name is Bobo the clown." "We have noticed you are a clown because of your red nose and white make up on your face" the children said. They all laughed but just then a bunch of seagulls came screaming towards them and pecked big holes in the clown's balloons and they started to collapse and shrink up and disintigrate. Luckily Luke and Kayla and Bobo were safe in the hot air balloon because the seagulls did not attack it. "Good thing you rescued me in time" said Bobo as they flew back to the beach. After they landed they said goodbye but they stayed friends and Bobo always gave the children balloons when he saw them and Kayla and Luke always asked him to their birthdays.

RATIONALE FOR GRADE 3 NARRATIVE WRITING MARK E

Score		Reporting Category
E	E	**Content:** **Events, actions, and ideas are consistently appropriate with the context established by the writer** (two children see a clown with balloons being lifted up into the air and flying away).
	E	**Details,** such as "They blew the biggest bubbles ever" and "They searched and searched the sky for the clown," **are specific and consistently effective and the reader is carried along with the efforts of the children to rescue the clown.**
	E	**The writing captivates the reader's interest and presents a well-supported main idea:** "let's try and rescue him and get him down."
E	E	**Organization:** **The beginning captures the reader's attention,** "'Look' screamed Luke to Kayla his best friend. 'What? Wow' cried Kayla. 'Look at all of the balloons and it looks like there's a clown hanging down from them.' 'Yeah your right' yelled Luke 'let's try and rescue him and get him down.' 'Okay' said Kayla," **clearly establishes events, characters, and setting and provides direction for the writing.**
	E	**Connections and/or relationships between events, actions, details, and characters are consistently maintained,** such as "They were too heavy for Luke's huba baba gum so they landed on the beach with a bump," "Luke and Kayla almost fell out of the basket as they helped the clown climb into it," and "Luke and Kayla and Bobo were safe in the hot air balloon because the seagulls did not attack it."
	E	**The ending,** "'Good thing you rescued me in time' said Bobo as they flew back to the beach. After they landed they said goodbye but they stayed friends and Bobo always gave the children balloons when he saw them and Kayla and Luke always asked him to their birthday party," **ties events and actions together.**

E		
		Sentence Structure:
	E	**Sentence structure is consistently controlled,** such as "They searched and searched the sky for the clown and a few hours later they saw him in the distance."
	E	**Sentence type and sentence length,** such as "'What? Wow' cried Kayla" and "After they landed they said goodbye but they stayed friends and Bobo always gave the children balloons when he saw them and Kayla and Luke always asked him to their birthday party," **are varied and effective.**
	E	**Sentence beginnings,** such as "It was a," "So on the," "Unfortunately it was not," and "Though it had been," **are consistently varied.**
		The length and complexity of the response has been considered.
E		**Vocabulary:**
	E	**Well-chosen words,** such as "grabbed her hand," "looked like a kite," and "red nose and white make up," **are used effectively.**
	E	**Expressions,** such as "'What? Wow,'" "her huba baba gum popped," "yelled 'Ahhhhhhhhh!'" and "seagulls came screaming towards them and pecked big holes," **are consistently precise and effective.**
	E	**Words and expressions,** such as "blew the biggest bubbles ever" and "collapse and shrink up and disintigrate," **are used to create vivid images and enhance the writing.**
		The length and complexity of the response has been considered.

		Conventions:
E	E	**End punctuation and capitalization are correct.**
	E	**Most words, familiar and unfamiliar, are spelled correctly,** such as "ocean" and "collapse." **Unfamiliar words,** such as "huba baba" and "disintigrate," **are spelled phonetically.**
	E	**Errors that are present,** such as "your right," **do not affect the clarity or effectiveness of communication.** **The length and complexity of the response has been considered.**

RESPONSES TO NARRATIVE WRITING PROMPT 3
SCORE S RESPONSE

The Bear

Once their were two children Millissa and Taylor. They were ahead of the family when they found a cave they were wondering what to do so they steped in and looked around and then sudenly the cave started to shakeing and then a huge boulder fell on the entrance. They were traped but they weren't very scared and they couldn't see a thing at all. They kept on walking. It started to get brighter and Tyler said "do you see that light?" "ya I do" said Millissa. They found a door. The door was very smooth and had a very big door knob. They where tierd and exsosting so they fell asleep. In the middle of the night something opened the door. Taylor was awake and went to see it. It had a hairy hand it was brown and had nails. The door opened a bit more Klang! Millissa woke up and Taylor wasn't their. "Taylor!" yelled Millissa. Nothing was their, then she knocked on the door nothing ansered. The rest of the family were looking for them. They looked at the cave and tried to move the rock but it was stuck. Down in the cave Millissa ran to the entrance "hello help me" "stay here I'll get help". Millissa looked back and saw a pair of red eyes she screamed. The firemen came just in time and opend the entrance and she ran out. "My friend is in there!" "he is in the bottom of the tunnel please help him" The firemen ran to the door and found Taylor. The firemen took them home and left the bear in the cave.

RATIONALE FOR GRADE 3 NARRATIVE WRITING MARK 3

Score		Reporting Category
S	S	**Content:** **The majority of the events, actions, and ideas are appropriate for the context established by the writer** (two children find a cave that they enter to explore).
	S	**Details,** such as "they steped in and looked around" and "Millissa ran to the entrance 'hello help me,'" **are general but appropriate for the story.**
	S	**The writing generally holds the reader's interest and provides some support for a main idea** as it tells how the children were trapped in the cave and were subsequently rescued.
S	S	**Organization:** **The beginning directly presents information about events, characters, and setting:** "Once their were two children Millissa and Taylor. They were ahead of the family when they found a cave they were wondering what to do so they steped in and looked around and then sudenly the cave started to shakeing and then a huge boulder fell on the entrance."
	S	**Connections and/or relationships between events, actions, details, and/or characters are generally maintained,** such as "they weren't very scared but they couldn't see a thing at all" and "The rest of the family were looking for them."
	S	**The ending,** "The firemen came just in time and opend the entrance and she ran out. 'My friend is in there!' 'he is in the bottom of the tunnel please help him'" The firemen ran to the door and found Taylor. The firemen took them home and left the bear in the cave," **is predictable and contrived but is connected to events and actions.**

S	S	**Sentence Structure:**
	S	**Sentence structure is generally controlled, but sentence run-ons may occasionally impeed the meaning,** such as "They were ahead of the family when they found a cave they were wondering what to do so they steped in and looked around and then sudenly the cave started to shakeing and then a huge boulder fell on the entrance."
	S	**Sentences may vary in type and length,** such as "They were traped but they weren't very scared and they couldn't see a thing at all" and "The rest of the family were looking for them."
		Some variety of sentence beginnings, such as "Once their were," "The door opened," and "Down in the cave," **is evident.**
		The length and complexity of the response has been considered.
S		**Vocabulary:**
	S	**Words chosen,** such as "wondering" and "something," **tend to be common or ordinary.**
	S	**Expressions,** such as "a huge boulder fell on the entrance" and "a hairy hand it was brown and had nails," **are usually more general than specific.**
	S	**Words and expressions,** such as "very smooth and had a very big door knob" and "Klang!" **sometimes enhance the writing.**
		The length and complexity of the response has been considered.

S	S	Conventions:
		Conventional end punctuation and capitalization are usually correct.
	S	Many familiar words, such as "ahead," "knocked," "entrance," and "tunnel," are spelled correctly; errors, such as "steped," "sudenly," "shakeing," and "ansered," suggest uneven control of spelling rules; unfamiliar words, such as "Millissa" and "exsosting," are generally spelled phonetically.
	S	Errors, such as "started to shakeing," "The found a," and "They where tierd and exsosting," are sometimes intrusive and may affect the clarity of communication.
		The length and complexity of the response has been considered.

SCORE PF RESPONSE

Lost

One day Jared and Emily walked to the park to play. When they got there Jared suggested to roll down the big hill. "Great idea" Emily said. They walked all the way up the hill and got ready to roll like a barell. But right before they said go Emily shouted out "look at that cave." They both ran to it and went inside not even bothering to look at the sign. They ran for 5 minutes and stopped at a dead end. "What a rip off" Jared moaned. "Let's go" Emily sighed but just as they started to leave Emily's foot lowered. She jumped up and found the tile had lowered and there was now an opening. They both stepped into the opening and were blinded by the sun. But it wasn't just the sun. A golden triangle bigger than a 23 story building was in front of them. The colosell building reflected the sun's rays. "I can't see" Jared yelled. "I'm blind" Emily screamed. "let's go into the building. There is a little hole we can squeeze through." "Man that's better," said Emily, "Where are we"? "Maybe in another demention" said Jared and Emily giggled.

They walked up to another door and went inside. Inside there was tons and tons of food. "Sweet," said Jared "I'm starving." They both ran up and started to munch. "I'm full" said Emily. "Me too" Jared moaned rubbing his tummy. "BOOM!!" "What's that?"cried Emily. "The ceiling is falling" yelled Jared. They ran as fast as they could to a far door and rushed out just as the ceiling came crashing down. "That was really close" said Jared. They turned around and gasped. There on bricks of gold in the middle of the room was a mummy. They started to go back but the mummy got up and began to chase them. "Run!" screamed Emily. They ran left, they ran right not knowing where to go. "There's the exit cried Jared." "It's closing" yelled Emily. "Slide!" screamed Jared. BOOM! The door shut. The mummy inside and Emily and Jared outside. "Let's get out of here" cried Jared.

As soon as they got to the park they ran home to tell mom what happened.

RATIONALE FOR GRADE 3 NARRATIVE WRITING MARK Pf

Score		Reporting Category
Pf	Pf Pf Pf	**Content:** **Events, actions, and ideas are intentionally chosen and are appropriate for the context established by the writer** (two children have an adventure after entering a cave on the side of a hill). **Details,** such as "Emily shouted out 'look at that cave'" and "the tile had lowered and there was now an opening," **are specific and generally effective.** **The writing is purposeful, draws the reader's interest and presents a supported main idea:** "ran to it and went inside not even bothering to look at the sign."
Pf	Pf Pf Pf	**Organization:** **The beginning,** "One day Jared and Emily walked to the park to play. When they got there Jared suggested to roll down the big hill. 'Great idea' Emily said. They walked all the way up the hill and got ready to roll like a barell. But right before they said go Emily shouted out 'look at that cave.' They both ran to it and went inside not even bothering to look at the sign," **clearly establishes events, characters, and setting and provides direction for the writing.** **Connections and/or relationships between events, actions, details, and characters are maintained,** such as "stepped into the opening and were blinded by the sun" and "tons and tons of food. 'Sweet,' said Jared 'I'm starving.'" **The ending,** "The door shut. The mummy inside and Emily and Jared outside. 'Let's get out of here' cried Jared. As soon as they got to the park they ran home to tell mom what happened," clearly **provides an appropriate finish for events and actions.**

Pf		**Sentence Structure:**
	Pf	**Sentence structure is controlled,** such as "When they got there Jared suggested to roll down the big hill."
	Pf	**Sentence type and sentence length,** such as "What's that?" and "There on bricks of gold in the middle of the room was a mummy," **are usually varied and effective.**
	Pf	**Sentence beginnings,** such as "One day," "But right before," and "A golden triangle," **are often varied.**
		The length and complexity of the response has been considered.
Pf		**Vocabulary:**
	Pf	**Well-chosen words,** such as "A golden triangle," "giggled," and "started to munch," **are often used.**
	Pf	**Expressions,** such as "'What a rip off' Jared moaned," "Emily sighed," "'Sweet,' said Jared 'I'm starving,'" and "They ran left, they ran right not knowing where to go," **are usually specific and effective.**
	Pf	**Words and expressions,** such as "roll like a barell," "colosell building reflected the sun's rays," and "BOOM! The door shut. The mummy inside and Emily and Jared outside," **are descriptive and often enhance the writing.**
		The length and complexity of the response has been considered.
Pf		**Conventions:**
	Pf	**End punctuation and capitalization are essentially correct.**
	Pf	**Familiar words are spelled correctly; errors,** such as "let's go" **are "slips";** unfamiliar words, such as "barell," "colosell," and "demention" **may be spelled phonetically.**
	Pf	**Errors that are present,** such as "a 23 story building" and "'There's the exit cried Jared,'" **rarely affect the clarity of communication.**
		The length and complexity of the response has been considered.

SCORE E RESPONSE

The Deserted Island

"Hey Kaya" I said "look at that cave." We raced inside and noticed that it was very dark and there was no noise. Kaya grabbed my arm as rocks began to cave in the entrance. We thought we were trapped so we walked deeper into the cave until at the very end we saw an exit. We ran out and discovered we were on an island. There were old houses and old cars on the streets. We ran into one house and Kaya held my hand. Slowly we walked from room to room but there was nobody there. We decided to go outside again and then we saw this old car. "Hey it's a mustang. Let's fix it and drive around" I said. After an hour it was fixed and we jumped in and I drove. We stopped at the biggest house we saw and ran in to explore. There was nobody around but there was masses of food. We grabbed as much as we could and put it into the car and drove off again. As we were almost out of gas we stopped at a gas station. "It looks old and it won't work" Kaya said but I pressed the pump and it worked. "They must have left not that long ago" I said. We drove off trying to catch up the people. There were lots and lots of trees but still there was the road through the trees. It was weird. We stopped and had some food and then we drove off again looking for somewhere to sleep.

Aventualy we came to a humungus mall. We slept in sleep country Canada. The next morning we went exploring. We found lots of food in the mall because of the food court and we stopped and had Mcdonalds. Then we ran around the mall getting clothes. I stopped at West 49 while Kaya ran to American Eagle. We then met at the car. It was very weird being the only ones on this huge island because there were cars and roads and malls and houses. Why did everyone leave? We had to find a way out of there but how? We drove and drove and drove and finally left the city. We came to a bridge to get off the island but there were lots of army men there. It was getting dark and one soldier stopped me. He said "Your not old enough to drive." "I know" I said as we got out of the car. "Why did you go into the cave? There was a notice that said keep out. I said "I don't know". He said to follow him so we did. He said some virus gave all the people in the island a bad flu and they died and now no one was allowed there. We got really scared and Kaya grabbed my hand again but he said we might not get the flu. The soldier gave us a ride home. My mom got really mad at me for going in the cave. The next day 2 more kids went in the cave and they never came BACK!

RATIONALE FOR GRADE 3 NARRATIVE WRITING MARK E

Score		Reporting Category
E		**Content:**
	E	Events, actions, and ideas are creative and are consistant with the context established by the writer (two children have a series of adventures after going into a cave that has a Do Not Enter sign).
	E	**Details,** such as "rocks began to cave in the entrance" and "I pressed the pump and it worked," **are precise and consistently effective** and the reader understands the strange experiences the writer is living through.
	E	**The writing is confident, holds the reader's interest and presents a well-supported main idea:** "We stopped and had some food and then we drove off again looking for somewhere to sleep."
E		**Organization:**
	E	**The beginning is purposeful,** "'Hey Kaya' I said " 'look at that cave.' We raced inside and noticed that it was very dark and there was no noise. Kaya grabbed my arm as rocks began to cave in the entrance. We thought we were trapped so we walked deeper into the cave until at the very end we saw an exit," **effectively establishes events, characters, and setting and provides direction for the writing.**
	E	**Connections and/or relationships between events, actions, details, and characters are developed and consistently maintained,** such as "As we were almost out of gas we stopped at a gas station," "We slept in sleep country Canada," and "very weird being the only ones on this huge island because there were cars and roads and malls and houses."
	E	**The ending,** "He said some virus gave all the people in the island a bad flu and they died and now no one was allowed there. We got really scared and Kaya grabbed my hand again but he said we might not get the flu. The soldier gave us a ride home. My mom got really mad at me for going in the cave. The next day 2 more kids went in the cave and they never came BACK!" effectively **ties events and actions together.**

E		**Sentence Structure:**
	E	**Sentence structure is consistently controlled,** such as "Slowly we walked from room to room but there was nobody there."
	E	**Sentence type and sentence length,** such as "We found lots of food in the mall because of the food court and we stopped and had Mcdonalds" and "Why did everyone leave?" **are varied and effective.**
	E	**Sentence beginnings,** such as "We raced," "Slowly we walked," "Aventualy we came," and "Why did," **are consistently varied.**
		The length and complexity of the response has been considered.
E		**Vocabulary:**
	E	**Well-chosen words,** such as "We grabbed" and "It was very weird," **are used effectively.**
	E	**Expressions,** such as "very dark and there was no noise," "I stopped at West 49 while Kaya ran to American Eagle," "some virus gave all the people in the island a bad flu," and "they never came BACK!" **are consistently precise and effective.**
	E	**Words and expressions,** such as "Hey it's a mustang" and "a humungus mall," **are used to create vivid images and enhance the writing.**
		The length and complexity of the response has been considered.

E		**Conventions:**
	E	**End punctuation and capitalization are correct.**
	E	**Most words, familiar and unfamiliar, are spelled correctly; spelling errors,** such as "Your not," **are understandable "slips."**
	E	**Errors that are present,** such as "was masses," "sleep country," and "We had to find a way out of there but how?" **do not affect the clarity or effectiveness of communication.**
		The length and complexity of the response has been considered.

UNIT TEST—WRITING

NARRATIVE WRITING PROMPT 1

DESCRIPTION

For this test you have 10 minutes for discussion, 10 minutes for planning, and 50 minutes to complete your writing. You may take up to 30 extra minutes to complete the test, if you need it.

INSTRUCTIONS

- Read the story starter as your teacher reads it aloud.

- Talk with your classmates about the writing activity or think about it by yourself.

- Plan your writing in whatever way you choose (web, list, pictures, etc.).

- Choose the kind of writing (story, letter, diary/journal entries) that will allow you to show your **best** writing.

- When you are doing your writing, print or write as neatly as you can.

- When you have finished, **check your work carefully** and correct any mistakes.

Look carefully at the picture. The children's horse has grown wings. Write an exciting story about what happens next.

_____

_____

_____

_____

_____

_____

_____

_____

SAMPLE RESPONSES

NARRATIVE WRITING

DESCRIPTION

For this test you have 10 minutes for discussion, 10 minutes for planning, and 50 minutes to complete your writing. You may take up to 30 extra minutes to complete the test, if you need it.

INSTRUCTIONS

Read the story starter as your teacher reads it aloud.

- Talk with your classmates about the writing activity or think about it by yourself.

- Plan your writing in whatever way you choose (web, list, pictures, etc.).

- Choose the kind of writing (story, letter, diary/journal entries) that will allow you to show your **best** writing.

- When you are doing your writing, print or write as neatly as you can.

- When you have finished, **check your work carefully** and correct any mistakes.

The Unicorn

One day when Billy and Maddy woke up got dressed and had breakfast. They went outside to feed there white horse but suddenly their horse had wings and it had a horn on its forhead. Billy said to Maddy what happend to our horse and what kind of creature is it. Maddy said it is a unicorn with wings on its side. Then Billy had a great idea Maddy said what is it Billy said why don't we ride the unicorn and travel around the world. Maddy said that would not be a good idea. Then Maddy said to Billy why dont we have it as our little secert. Billy agreed. The next day while Maddy was eating her breakfast Billy went outside to check on there unicorn. But suddenly Billy saw that the unicorn was gone so Billy quickly called Maddy. Maddy put her shoes on and ran quicly outside the door. Maddy asked Billy where is our unicorn Billy answered in a worried vocice the unicorn ran away from home to look for food so it could eat. Maddy said lets go in to the woods and look our white horned unicorn. Billy said that is a great idea so together they went looking for there unicorn. In the middle of the woods they found their unicorn and they took it back home.

RATIONALE FOR GRADE 3 NARRATIVE WRITING MARKS S

Score		Reporting Category
S		**Content:**
	S	**The majority of the events, actions, and ideas are appropriate for the context established by the writer** (two children discover that their horse has grown wings).
	S	**Details are general but appropriate for the story,** such as "they went outside to feed there white horse" and "it is a unicorn with wings on its side."
	S	**The writing generally holds the reader's interest and provides some support for a main idea** as it tells what the children thought when they discovered that their horse had turned into a unicorn.
S		**Organization:**
	S	**The beginning,** "One day when Billy and Maddy woke up got dressed and had breakfast. They went outside to feed there white horse but suddenly their horse had wings and it had a horn on its forhead," **directly presents information about events, characters, and setting.**
	S	**Connections and/or relationships between events, actions, details, and/or characters are generally maintained,** such as "ride the unicorn and travel around the world" and "the unicorn ran away from home to look for food."
	S	**The ending,** "Maddy said lets go in to the woods and look our white horned unicorn. Billy said that is a great idea so together they went looking for there unicorn. In the middle of the woods they found their unicorn and they took it back home," **is predictable but is connected to events and actions.**

S		
		Sentence Structure:
	S	**Sentence structure is generally controlled, but sentence run-ons may occasionally impede the meaning,** such as "Then Billy had a great idea Maddy said what is it Billy said why don't we ride the unicorn and travel around the world."
	S	**Sentences may vary in type and length,** such as "Billy agreed" and "The next day while Maddy was eating her breakfast Billy went outside to check on there unicorn."
	S	**Some variety of sentence beginnings,** such as "One day," "But suddenly," and "Maddy asked," **is evident.**
		The length and complexity of the response has been considered.
S		**Vocabulary:**
	S	**Words chosen,** such as "woke up got dressed and had breakfast" and "was gone," **tend to be common or ordinary.**
	S	**Expressions,** such as "had a great idea" and "answered in a worried vocice," **are usually more general than specific.**
	S	**Words and expressions,** such as "little secert" and "our white horned unicorn," **sometimes enhance the writing.**
		The length and complexity of the response has been considered.

S		Conventions:
	S	Conventional end punctuation and capitalization are usually correct.
	S	Many familiar words, such as "suddenly," "unicorn," "idea," and "worried," are spelled correctly; errors, such as "there," "happend," "don't," "secret," "quicly," and "vocice," suggest uneven control of spelling rules; unfamiliar words, such as "forhead," are generally spelled phonetically.
	S	Errors, such as "why do we ride the unicorn," "The Maddy said," and "and look our white horned unicorn," are sometimes intrusive and may affect the clarity of communication.
		The length and complexity of the response has been considered.

SCORE PF RESPONSE

The Magical Adventure

Another normal day for Nick and Lisa. Little did they know that the day would be different from any other day of their lives. Nick is 10 and Lisa is 9 years old. When they both go outside to play they notice something strange happening to their horse. They run to the fence and climb upon it. Their horse is growing wings! They keep watching while their horse grows more and more like a unicorn. Nick is different from most boys because he likes fairy tales and things like that and so he was amazed just as much as Lisa was. "LOOK!" said Lisa because by now their horse had completly turned into a unicorn, even the colour! The next day Lisa and Nick go outside to see their unicorn. She was standing in the exact same spot as last night. Yesterday they had said they would try to talk to her so they snuck up beside her and said hi. What a surprise when the unicorn said hi back. "Wow you can talk" said Nick and Lisa at the same time. They talked for a while and then the unicorn said "Would you like a ride?" "Of course" said Lisa. "That would be great" said Nick. Next thing they knew they were riding on the back of a unicorn, flying across the city! On the ride they see cool places like their home and the playground and their school. "Everything looks different from up here" said Nick. Soon after they were back home and the unicorn said "You should go back home now. But first I have to tell you that I only turn into a unicorn 1 time a year and you are very lucky kids." "Will we see you again next year?" asked Lisa."

"Of course! I live here, remember?"

"Yea. We just forgot, we had so much fun with you."

"You two should get going now."

"Your right." "Bye!"

RATIONALE FOR GRADE 3 NARRATIVE WRITING MARKS PF

Score		Reporting Category
Pf		**Content:**
	Pf	**Events, actions, and ideas are appropriate for the context established by the writer** (two children discover that their horse has grown wings and turned into a unicorn).
	Pf	**Details,** such as "their horse grows more and more like a unicorn," "they snuck up beside her and said hi," and "flying across the city!" **are specific and generally effective.**
	Pf	**The writing engages the reader's interest and presents a supported main idea:** "Their horse is growing wings!"
Pf		**Organization:**
	Pf	**The beginning,** "Another normal day for Nick and Lisa. Little did they know that the day would be different from any other day of their lives. Nick is 10 and Lisa is 9 years old. When they both go outside to play they notice something strange happening to their horse," **clearly establishes events, characters, and setting and provides direction for the writing.**
	Pf	**Connections and/or relationships between events, actions, details, and characters are maintained,** such as "Nick is different from most boys," "the unicorn said 'Would you like a ride?'" and "'Everything looks different from up here.'"
	Pf	**The ending,** "Soon after they were back home and the unicorn said 'You should go back home now. But first I have to tell you that I only turn into a unicorn 1 time a year and you are very lucky kids.' 'Will we see you again next year?' asked Lisa. 'Of course! I live here, remember?' 'Yea. We just forgot, we had so much fun with you.' 'You two should get going now.' 'Your right.' 'Bye!'" **provides an appropriate finish for the events and actions.**

Pf		**Sentence Structure:**
	Pf	**Sentence structure is controlled,** such as "They keep watching while their horse grows more and more like a unicorn."
	Pf	**Sentence type and sentence length,** such as "Their horse is growing wings!" and "Nick is different from most boys because he likes fairy tales and things like that and so he was amazed just as much as Lisa was," **are usually varied and effective.**
	Pf	**Sentence beginnings,** such as "Nick is different," "Yesterday they had," "What a surprise," and "But first I," **are often varied.**
		The length and complexity of the response has been considered.
Pf		**Vocabulary:**
	Pf	**Well-chosen words,** such as "they snuck up" and "see cool places," **are often used.**
	Pf	**Expressions,** such as "flying across the city!" and "Everything looks different from up here," **are usually specific and effective.**
	Pf	**Words and expressions,** such as "the day would be different from any other day of their lives," "'LOOK!'" and "'Wow you can talk' said Nick and Lisa at the same time," **are descriptive and often enhance the writing.**
		The length and complexity of the response has been considered.
Pf		**Conventions:**
	Pf	**End punctuation and capitalization are essentially correct.**
	Pf	**Familiar words are spelled correctly; spelling errors,** such as "completly," **are "slips."**
	Pf	**Errors that are present,** such as the sentence fragment, "Another normal day for Nick and Lisa," the frequent tense changes within a sentence, and "Your right," **rarely affect the clarity of communication.**
		The length and complexity of the response has been considered.

SCORE E RESPONSE

One Chance

It was a beautiful August day, 31 degrees C. to be exact and me and Kyle were going out for our morning ride when suddenly I heard Kyle yell at me to come quickly. I ran as fast as I could to see that our full grown male horse had grown stubs of wings off the tips of his shoulders. Now we were both standing on top of the fence when I asked Kyle "When did Star begin to grow wings?" "I have no idea Anna," he told me and that's when I remembered something I had read once about winged horses. "Kyle we have to go inside" I whispered to him urgently. So on the walk back to the house I told him about how winged horses needed to eat the fruit of a Plora tree or his wings would not grow in properly and be half normal, half not. That's when our adventure began! Luckily mom and dad were both away on business trips so we could help Star become a winged horse. The problem was if he did not eat the fruit in time his chances would be up. So we rushed back to the field, hopped on Star's back and rode for about 4 hours straight. Soon it was night and we had to stop under a tree and rest. Unfortunately it was not a Plora tree but it gave us shade. When we woke up the next morning to our surprise there was a circus no more than 200 metres away. We decided to have a break so we went over to the circus. First we went on the fairis wheel Star waited at the bottom. Next we decided to go on the caracel because Star was aloud on if he stood still. We climbed on and it started off slow but after a few seconds it got faster and faster and faster until we could not hang on. The ride had malfunctioned and me, Kyle and Star were thrown off balance and out the door of the ride. Luckily we were not hurt bad so we only had to go to the medic tent to get some bandages. Soon we were aloud to leave and we were moaning and groaning but Kyle and me knew Star's time was running out. We hopped on his back again and continued riding west in search of a Plora tree. As we rode we did not know the Queen's castle was in front of us. When we reached the castle we had to pay to get past but we did not think to bring any money so we had to make a promise. Star promised that the first child that was born of his wife would be given to the Queen. So it was done we had made our promise and we were on our way again. Though it had been a hard long journey we at last found a Plora tree. As soon as we fed the fruit to Star and had a little ourselves we fell asleep and when we woke up we were at home lying under Star's big beautiful wings.

RATIONALE FOR GRADE 3 NARRATIVE WRITING MARKS E

Score		Reporting Category
E		**Content:**
	E	**Events, actions, and ideas are creative and consistant with the context established by the writer** (two children discover that their horse has grown wings and they set off to ensure that the wings grow properly).
	E	**Details,** such as "I remembered something I had read once about winged horses" and "we rushed back to the field, hopped on Star's back and rode for about 4 hours," **are precise and consistently effective** and the reader is carried along in the search for the Plora tree.
	E	**The writing is confident, holds the reader's interest, and presents a well-supported main idea:** "The problem was if he did not eat the fruit in time his chances would be up."
E		**Organization:**
	E	**The beginning captures the reader's attention,** "It was a beautiful August day, 31 degrees C. to be exact and me and Kyle were going out for our morning ride when suddenly I heard Kyle yell at me to come quickly. I ran as fast as I could to see that our full grown male horse had grown stubs of wings off the tips of his shoulders. Now we were both standing on top of the fence when I asked Kyle 'When did Star begin to grow wings?'" **clearly and effectively establishes events, characters, and setting and provides direction for the writing.**
	E	**Connections and/or relationships between events, actions, details, and characters are developed and consistently maintained,** such as "We decided to have a break so we went over to the circus," "Kyle and me knew Star's time was running out," and "we had to pay to get past but we did not think to bring any money."
	E	**The ending,** "Though it had been a hard long journey we at last found a Plora tree. As soon as we fed the fruit to Star and had a little ourselves we fell asleep and when we woke up we were at home lying under Star's big beautiful wings," **effectively ties events and actions together.**

E		**Sentence Structure:**
	E	**Sentence structure is consistently controlled,** such as "'I have no idea Anna,' he told me and that's when I remembered something I had read once about winged horses."
	E	**Sentence type and sentence length,** such as "That's when our adventure began!" and "We climbed on and it started off slow but after a few seconds it got faster and faster and faster until we could not hang on," **are varied and effective.**
	E	**Sentence beginnings,** such as "It was a," "So on the," "Unfortunately it was not," and "Though it had been," **are consistently varied.**
		The length and complexity of the response has been considered.
E		**Vocabulary:**
	E	**Well-chosen words,** such as "malfunctioned" and "moaning and groaning," **are used effectively.**
	E	**Expressions,** such as "whispered to him urgently," "it gave us shade," "faster and faster and faster until we could not hang on," and "a hard long journey," **are consistently precise and effective.**
	E	**Words and expressions,** such as "stubs of wings off the tips of his shoulders" and "lying under Star's big beautiful wings," **are used to create vivid images and enhance the writing.**
		The length and complexity of the response has been considered.
E		**Conventions:**
	E	**End punctuation and capitalization are correct.**
	E	**Most words, familiar and unfamiliar, are spelled correctly,** such as "malfunctioned" and "journey." The words "fairis wheel" and "caracel" **are spelled phonetically.**
	E	**Errors that are present,** such as "me and Kyle," "were aloud," and "were not hurt bad," **do not affect the clarity or effectiveness of communication.**
		The length and complexity of the response has been considered.

NOTES

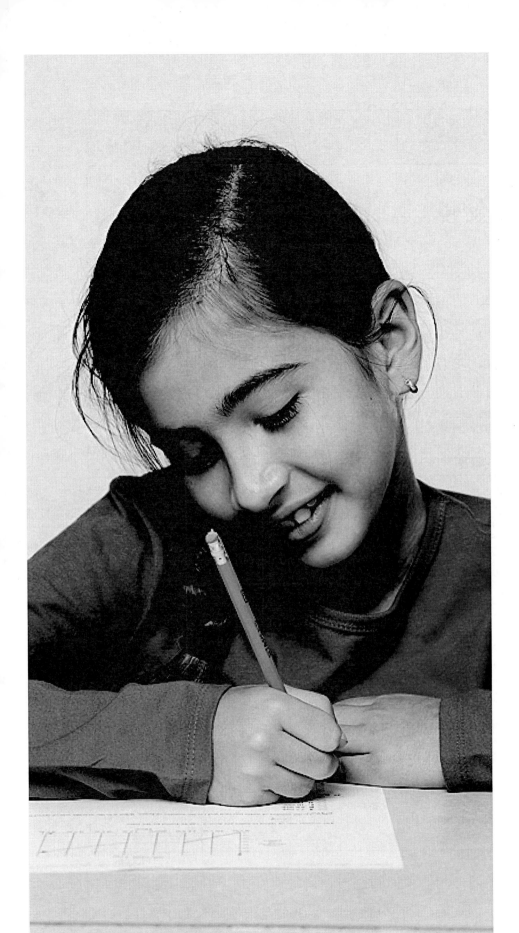

Part B: Provincial
Achievement Tests

TABLE OF CORRELATIONS			
General Outcome	**Specific Outcome**	**2000 Achievement Test**	**2001 Achievement test**
Students are expected to …			
2.1 Use strategies and cues	2.1.1.2 identify the different ways in which oral, print and other media texts, such as stories, textbooks, letters, pictionaries and junior dictionaries, are organized	9	
	2.1.2.2 apply a variety of strategies, such as setting a purpose, confirming predictions, making inferences and drawing conclusions	4, 7, 12, 14, 15, 16, 17, 18, 29, 33, 37	6, 19, 20, 23, 36
	2.1.2.3 identify the main idea or topic and supporting details in simple narrative and expository passages	2, 34, 40	2, 3
	2.1.2.4 extend sight vocabulary to include predictable phrases and words related to language use	1, 10, 19	
	2.1.2.6 monitor and confirm meaning by rereading when necessary, and by applying knowledge of pragmatic, semantic, syntactic and graphophonic cueing systems	6, 28, 39	22
2.2 Respond to Texts	2.2.2.2 summarize the main idea of individual oral, print and other media texts	35	
	2.2.2.4 make inferences about characters' actions or feelings	24, 25, 26	5, 8, 21
	2.2.3.2 identify how authors use comparisons, and explain how they create mental images		39

2.3 Understand forms, elements and techniques	2.3.1.2 discuss ways that visual images convey meaning in print and other media texts	20, 21, 23	4
	2.3.2.1 include evnts, setting and characters when summarizing or retelling oral, print, or other media texts	38	
	2.3.2.3 identify ways that messages are enhanced in oral, print, and other media texts by the use of specific techniques	31	7
	2.3.3.1 recognize examples of repeated humour, sound and poetic effects that contribute to audience enjoyment	32	9
3.1 Plan and focus	3.1.1.2 identify facts and opinions, main ideas and details in oral, print and other media texts		38
3.2 Select and process	3.2.1.1 find information to answer research questions, using a variety of sources, such as children's magazines, CDROMs, plays, folk tales, songs, stories and the environment		37
	3.2.2.2 locate answers to questions and extract appropriate and significant information from oral, print and other media texts	3, 5, 8, 11, 13, 22, 27, 30, 36	1, 40

NOTES

2000 PROVINCIAL ACHIEVEMENT TEST

ENGLISH LANGUAGE ARTS

PART B: READING

Description:

This test has 2 sections:

1) Section A has 5 selections and 23 questions.

2) Section B has 4 selections and 17 questions.

You have 60 minutes to complete this test. Your teacher will give you a break between Section A and Section B. You may take up to 30 extra minutes to complete this test.

Instructions:

– You will need a pencil and eraser. Use only an HB pencil.

– Read each selection carefully. Read each question carefully.

– You may underline any key words in the passage or question that may help you.

– Choose the best or correct answer.

– Mark your answer in this booklet by filling in the circle next to your answer. Look at the example below to see how to mark your answer.

– If you want to change an answer, erase your first mark completely.

– When you are finished the test, go back and check that you did each question. You may want to read each selection again.

Example Question

Rex is a big dinosaur. He is taller than a giraffe.
Rex is as tall as a house!

1) Rex is a

    Ⓐ   pet

    Ⓑ   bird

    Ⓒ   giraffe

    ●   dinosaur

SECTION A

I. **Read the following story and answer questions 1 to 4.**

from **Belle's Journey**

Every Saturday on the great wide prairie, Molly rode her brown mare Belle to piano lessons. Eight miles to the piano teacher's house and eight miles home.

On hot summer days they rode under a high yellow sun and a blue sky. In winter they trudged along the trails beneath grey skies and a low pale sun that gave no warmth.

Molly rode bareback, as there was no money for a saddle. Sometimes in winter when the trails were rough, she would slip and tumble off the horse's back into the snow. When that happened, Belle always stopped and turned her long, kind face around to see if Molly was all right. Then the mare would wait patiently while the little girl scrambled up onto her back again before she resumed her slow, measured gait along the trail.

Marilynn Reynolds

1. **In the title, the word "Journey" means**

    Ⓐ riding bareback

    Ⓑ riding a horse

    Ⓒ accident

    Ⓓ long trip

2. **Molly rode Belle to**

    Ⓐ her teacher's house

    Ⓑ her uncle's stable

    Ⓒ the open prairie

    Ⓓ the rough trails

3. **Belle turned to see if Molly was all right each time Molly**

    Ⓐ rode on the great wide prairie

    Ⓑ went to the piano teacher's house

    Ⓒ tumbled off the horse's back

    Ⓓ scrambled onto the horse's back

4. **A word that describes Belle is**

    Ⓐ clumsy

    Ⓑ patient

    Ⓒ poor

    Ⓓ thin

II.   Read the following story and answer questions 5 to 8.

from **Two Bad Ants**

When the ants came out of the tunnel they found themselves in a strange world. Smells they had known all their lives, smells of dirt and grass and rotting plants, had vanished. There was no more wind and, most puzzling of all, it seemed that the sky was gone.

They crossed smooth shiny surfaces, then followed the scout up a glassy, curved wall. They had reached their goal. From the top of the wall they looked below to a sea of crystals. One by one the ants climbed down into the sparkling treasure.

Quickly they each chose a crystal, then turned to start the journey home. There was something about this unnatural place that made the ants nervous. In fact they left in such a hurry that none of them noticed the two small ants who stayed behind.

"Why go back?" one asked the other. "This place may not feel like home, but look at all these crystals." "You're right," said the other, "we can stay here and eat this tasty treasure every day, forever." So the two ants ate crystal after crystal until they were too full to move, and fell asleep.

Chris Van Allsburg

ELA3/9903 Ants

5. **One of the reasons that the ants were puzzled was that**

Ⓐ   they were very lost

Ⓑ   the crystals sparkled

Ⓒ   their tunnel was dark

Ⓓ   the usual smells had disappeared

6. **The underlined word** <u>scout</u> **means**

Ⓐ   trail

Ⓑ   track

Ⓒ   smell

Ⓓ   leader

7. **The two ants who stayed behind were not noticed by the other ants because the other ants were**

Ⓐ   busy picking up crystals

Ⓑ   hidden by the crystals

Ⓒ   leaving too quickly

Ⓓ   in a dark place

8. **The two small ants decided to stay so that they could**

Ⓐ   eat the tasty treasure

Ⓑ   move more crystals

Ⓒ   feel at home

Ⓓ   fall asleep

III. Read the following recipe and answer questions 9 to 13.

from **A Pioneer Story**

Dried apple slices make good snacks. Try some yourself.

– You'll need:

– a peeler

– 2 or 3 apples

– a paring knife

– cookie sheets

1. Peel the apples. Ask an adult to cut them into quarters, remove the core and slice the quarters into thin slices.

2. Spread the slices on the cookie sheets so that the slices do not overlap.

3. Turn the oven to 70°C (150°F). Wearing oven mitts, place the trays of apple slices in the oven.

4. Your apple slices will take six hours or longer to dry. Once every hour, take the cookie sheets out of the oven and turn the slices so they will dry evenly, then put them back in the oven. Always use oven mitts when handling the cookie sheets.

5. At the end of six hours, take two slices out of the oven and let them cool. Test the slices by squeezing them. If they leave moisture on your fingers, they are not yet dry. Leave the cookie sheets in for another hour and test again.

6. Store the dried fruit in tightly covered containers or plastic bags. Eat the slices as snacks or add them to your morning cereal.

Barbara Greenwood

9. **Before drying the apples, you must first**

   Ⓐ peel, slice, turn, and squeeze the apples

   Ⓑ peel, quarter, core, and slice the apples

   Ⓒ peel, spread, turn, and store the apples

   Ⓓ peel, core, slice, and cover the apples

10. **When an apple is cut into quarters, there are**

    Ⓐ 8 pieces

    Ⓑ 6 pieces

    Ⓒ 4 pieces

    Ⓓ 2 pieces

11. **After you put the slices in the oven, they should be turned every**

    Ⓐ hour

    Ⓑ half-hour

    Ⓒ six hours

    Ⓓ seven hours

12. **When handling the cookie sheets, you should use oven mitts because if you do not, your hands will**

    Ⓐ get covered

    Ⓑ get burned

    Ⓒ be dirty

    Ⓓ be wet

13. **To tell if the apple slices are dry, you should**

    Ⓐ squeeze them

    Ⓑ taste them

    Ⓒ cool them

    Ⓓ turn them

IV. **Read the following story and answer questions 14 to 18.**
from **Squiggle and the Giant**

Squiggle squirmed along happily in the soft, muddy soil. Then he felt a hard, rough surface beneath him. He remembered Grandfather's warning. "This must be pavement," he thought. "It doesn't feel very dangerous to me." He slithered into a puddle on the pavement to play.

Squiggle had fun wiggling and twisting in the puddle. He didn't notice when the water stopped falling. He didn't notice the air getting warmer. He didn't notice the puddle getting smaller . . . and smaller. Then the puddle was gone.

Squiggle lay on the hot pavement. His dry skin no longer glistened. He tried to burrow into the pavement, but it was too hard. He tried to wiggle off the pavement, but his skin could not slip over the rough surface. He could hardly move.

The ground began to tremble. A giant must be coming!
Squiggle felt himself being lifted high into the sky by one of the giant people!

"Silly worm," boomed the giant's voice. "Don't you know it's dangerous for worms to be on the sidewalk?"

The giant put Squiggle down on the dirt. Squiggle burrowed into the soft, moist earth, and the giant climbed onto her tricycle and rode away.

D.A. Woodliff

14. **Grandfather had warned Squiggle about**

    Ⓐ   puddles

    Ⓑ   pavement

    Ⓒ   muddy soil

    Ⓓ   giant people

15. **The puddle probably got smaller because**

    Ⓐ   the giant splashed the water away

    Ⓑ   there was a hole in the pavement

    Ⓒ   the air got hotter

    Ⓓ   it got filled with mud

16. **After the puddle disappeared, Squiggle could not move because**

    Ⓐ   the water made him too slippery

    Ⓑ   he was too afraid of the giant

    Ⓒ   the pavement was too hard

    Ⓓ   his skin was too dry

17. Squiggle thought that a giant was coming because he

    (A)   remembered his grandfather's warning

    (B)   noticed the puddle getting smaller

    (C)   heard a booming voice

    (D)   felt the ground move

18. The next time Squiggle feels pavement, he will MOST LIKELY

    (A)   wiggle back to soft earth

    (B)   play in a puddle

    (C)   look for a giant

    (D)   burrow into it

V.   Read the following information and answer questions 19 to 23.

After a lot of digging, a scientist has found many fossil clues in some rocks. These clues tell about what happened here long ago. Read the story.

from **Rock Read**

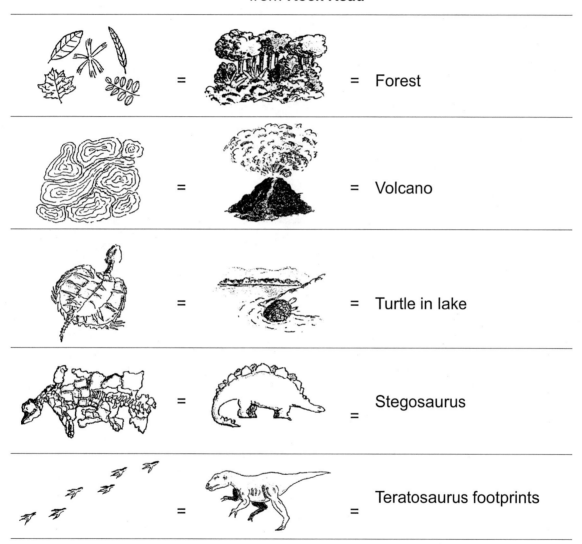

Long ago, a left its in the mud. Years and years

passed, and then a died here. Millions of years later, a

 formed where the and  had once

lived, and a came to live in it. One day, a

erupted and filled the 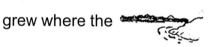 with lava and ash. And after a long

time, a 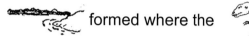 grew where the  had once been.

19. The words that BEST show when this story takes place are

Ⓐ "Long ago"

Ⓑ "years passed"

Ⓒ "One day"

Ⓓ "once been"

20. In this story, which dinosaur died <u>here</u>?

Ⓐ Stegosaurus

Ⓑ Teratosaurus

Ⓒ Tyrannosaurus

Ⓓ Edmontonsaurus

21. Which of the following pictures shows what lived in the lake?

Ⓐ

Ⓑ

Ⓒ

Ⓓ

22. After the volcano erupted,

    Ⓐ   turtles came to the forest

    Ⓑ   a forest grew by the lake

    Ⓒ   dinosaurs left their footprints

    Ⓓ   the lake filled with lava and ash

23. Where the lake had once been, after a long time, there was a

    Ⓐ   fossil

    Ⓑ   forest

    Ⓒ   volcano

    Ⓓ   mountain

SECTION B

VI. **Read the following story and answer questions 24 to 27.**

from **The Wing Shop**

A very thin little girl with red fuzzy hair stood on a stool dusting a pair of chicken wings.

"Hello," said the girl. "My name is Lucy Featherman, may I help you?"

"Yes," replied Matthew, "I need a pair of wings."

"We've got plenty of those," Lucy said. "What kind do you need?"

"Well, I don't know," said Matthew. "Do you have a pair that can get me back to Main Street?"

The girl frowned and looked around the store. "I really don't know," she explained. "You see, I'm just watching the store for my grandfather. He went out to test some firefly wings last night and hasn't come back yet. Why don't you try on a pair?"

Matthew decided on a pair of lovely gray and white ones.

"Oh, you look wonderful," Lucy told him. "But don't you want to take off your socks and shoes?"

Just as Matthew bent down to untie his sneakers, a great gust of wind from an open window picked him up, and his wings began to flap! Before he knew it, he was flying out of the shop!

"Oh well, that's a good idea," said Lucy. "Go for a test flight and see if you like them. Don't worry, they're guaranteed to bring you back."

ELA3/9903 Angle

But Matthew was worried! He had never flown before, and it felt very strange to be so far off the ground! He was flying high above the city's buildings. "This doesn't seem like the way back to Main Street," Matthew thought as he headed out to the harbor.

Elvira Woodruff

24. Matthew asked for wings so that he could

Ⓐ find Lucy's grandfather

Ⓑ return to Main Street

Ⓒ get to the harbour

Ⓓ go flying again

25. Matthew picked out his own pair of wings because Lucy

Ⓐ was too busy to help

Ⓑ was too small to reach the wings

Ⓒ didn't know much about wings

Ⓓ didn't know where Main Street was

26. Matthew was worried that he was flying in the wrong direction because he was

Ⓐ high above the city's building

Ⓑ flying toward the harbour

Ⓒ flying out of the shop

Ⓓ so far off the ground

27. **The wings Matthew put on were PROBABLY those of a**

Ⓐ   crow

Ⓑ   chicken

Ⓒ   sea gull

Ⓓ   penguin

VII. **Read the following information and answer questions 28 to 30.**

from **Giants of the Forest**

Redwoods are the tallest trees in the world. The tallest redwood is taller than a twenty-story building. It is so big around that six people holding hands could barely reach around it.

How do redwoods get so big? First, they live where the weather is just right for them. Redwood trees grow near the Pacific Ocean in the states of California and Oregon. They live in an area with hot dry summers and warm rainy winters... Though they don't get much rain, fog comes in every day, and the trees get water from the fog. And redwoods are not hurt by pests. Redwoods have very thick bark, so insects can't hurt the inside of the trees.

Even fire does not hurt redwood trees. Redwoods have three ways to guard against forest fires. First, their bark must get very hot in order to burn. Next, the needles and branches, which burn more easily than the bark, are far up from the ground. Fire almost never reaches them. And because redwood branches keep the sunlight from getting to the forest floor, not many plants can grow under redwoods. So fires don't start easily in the forest.

It's a good thing redwoods are so healthy, for they take many years to grow... they often live and keep growing for two thousand years! They are some of the oldest living things in the world.

28.The underlined word <u>barely</u> means

    Ⓐ   never

    Ⓑ   easily

    Ⓒ   hardly

    Ⓓ   always

29. Few plants grow around redwoods because the

    Ⓐ   insects eat them

    Ⓑ   forest fires burn them

    Ⓒ   weather is too cold for them

    Ⓓ   ground around them is shaded

30. Redwoods live to be some of the world's oldest living things because they are

    Ⓐ   very tall

    Ⓑ   so healthy

    Ⓒ   big around

    Ⓓ   near the ocean

VIII.   **Read the following poem and answer questions 31 to 35.**

My Toboggan and I Carve Winter

My toboggan and I carve winter

We crunch over the powdery snow

the one by one glistening grains

they sigh and squeek

then RACE

faster and faster

<u>whipping the wind</u> apart
carving jet trails with swirling tails

circling the shadow of every tree

<u>nearing full flight</u>

till

WHOMP!

a lurking bump tumbles us

into the drifts of freezing snow

We trudge slowly skyward for another run.

by Jane Wadley

31. **The words RACE and WHOMP are PROBABLY printed in capital letters to**

    Ⓐ show an exciting action

    Ⓑ describe a loud noise

    Ⓒ describe the snow

    Ⓓ show the winner

32. **The author uses the underlined words whipping the wind to describe a**

    Ⓐ freezing day

    Ⓑ tree bending

    Ⓒ scarf trailing behind

    Ⓓ tobbogan going fast

33. **When nearing full flight, the child in the poem would probably feel**

    Ⓐ sad

    Ⓑ bored

    Ⓒ lonely

    Ⓓ thrilled

34. **The child tumbles into the drift because of the**

(A) powdery snow

(B) whipping wind

(C) shadowy trees

(D) lurking bump

35. Another good title for this poem would be

(A) Winter Fun

(B) Powdery Snow

(C) The Big Freeze

(D) My Friends and I

IX. Read the following story and answer questions 36 to 40.

from **The Watcher**

George was a watcher. He watched TV. He watched cars, trucks and big machines. George watched clouds in summer . . . and snow falling in winter. George loved to watch shoppers at the mall and birds at the bird feeder. . .

One Monday at noon, George sat quietly eating his lunch, watching the helpers dish out macaroni and hot dogs, watching orange juice rising up through drinking straws, watching the kids trade their desserts and watching the rain stream down the windows.

Suddenly, from across the room, George noticed Sarah, a girl from his class. She was clutching her throat and staring wildly at the kids around her.

"Sarah!" yelled George. . .

George saw the school nurse walking in the hall. George sprang out of his seat, jumped over two tables and shouted, in his loudest voice, "Miss Clayton!"

The nurse stopped and looked at George.

"Sarah's choking!" yelled George. He pointed at her.

Miss Clayton ran to Sarah. She knew just what to do.

When Sarah was breathing again, Miss Clayton led her away.

Everyone looked at George.

"It's a good thing you were here, George," said Dan.

"I saw a safety show on TV," said George. "It said to stay calm and take charge. So I did."

The kids all slapped George on the back and said, "Great!" and "Excellent!"…

Brenda Silsbe

36. **In the story, one thing George loved to watch was**

   Ⓐ   shoppers at the mall

   Ⓑ   children in the park

   Ⓒ   animals at the zoo

   Ⓓ   kites in the sky

37. **When George saw Sarah clutching her throat, he PROBABLY felt**

   Ⓐ   excited

   Ⓑ   scared

   Ⓒ   proud

   Ⓓ   sick

38. **This story takes place in a**

   Ⓐ   store

   Ⓑ   house

   Ⓒ   school

   Ⓓ   restaurant

39. The words George sprang out of his seat mean that George

Ⓐ   shouted loudly

Ⓑ   jumped up quickly

Ⓒ   slid under the table

Ⓓ   bounced around the room

40. What is the lesson in this story?

Ⓐ   Watching can be helpful

Ⓑ   Always eat your lunch

Ⓒ   Help the school nurse

Ⓓ   Watch more TV

ANSWERS AND SOLUTIONS—2000 PROVINCIAL ACHIEVEMENT TEST

1. D	9. B	17. D	25. C	33. D
2. A	10. C	18. A	26. B	34. C
3. C	11. A	19. A	27. C	35. A
4. B	12. B	20. A	28. C	36. A
5. D	13. A	21. A	29. D	37. B
6. D	14. B	22. D	30. B	38. C
7. C	15. C	23. B	31. A	39. B
8. A	16. D	24. B	32. D	40. A

SECTION A

Belle's Journey

1. D

This is a story about a girl named Molly and her horse, Belle. Molly rides Belle to the piano teacher's house. It is eight miles to the piano teacher's house. So, the story "Belle's Journey" is about the long trip that Molly and Belle take when they go to the piano teacher's house.

2. A

The first and second lines of the story state that Molly rode her horse to piano lessons. The piano lessons were at the teacher's house. So, Molly rode to her teacher's house.

3. C

In the last paragraph, it is stated that sometimes Molly would tumble off the horse's back. The next sentence tells us that when Molly fell off, Belle would stop and look around to see if Molly was all right.

4. B

In the last sentence of the story, it is stated that "the mare would wait patiently." The word that describes Belle is "patient." There is nothing in the story that shows that Belle is clumsy, poor, or thin.

Two Bad Ants

5. D

The ants were not lost or puzzled by the way the crystals sparkled because it was their goal to come out of the tunnel and find these crystals. The tunnel was dark, but the ants were used to darkness because they live underground.

The story says that the "Smells they had known all their lives … had vanished." The ants were puzzled because the smells they were used to had disappeared.

6. D

This was the ants' first journey out of the tunnel, so the word "scout" could not mean *trail* or *track*. A trail or track is made after someone or something has already taken a route. The word *smell* is also incorrect. The second line in the story says that all the smells the ants knew had vanished. The story does not mention any other smells that the ants would follow. The word "scout" means *leader*. The ants followed the leader up the wall.

7. C

The sea of crystals was very sparkly. It was not at all a dark place like the tunnel.

The other ants may have been busy picking up crystals and they may have been hidden behind crystals; however, the reason the other ants did not notice the two that stayed behind is that the place made the other ants feel nervous and they left too quickly.

8. A

The ants did not fall asleep until after they had eaten many crystals. The ants were not trying to move more crystals. If they had been, they would have been going as fast as the other ants. The two small ants that stayed behind were greedy. The third sentence in the fourth paragraph gives the answer to the question. The ants decided to stay so they could "eat this tasty treasure every day, forever."

A Pioneer Story

9. B

The answer to this question is found listed in the first direction: first, the apples must be peeled. The next step is to cut the apples into quarters. Then, remove the core. Finally, the apples can be cut into thin slices.

10. C

When a whole apple is cut into quarters, it is cut into four pieces. If an apple is cut into two equal pieces, it is cut in half. If an apple is cut into 6 pieces, each piece is a sixth of the apple. When an apple is cut into 8 pieces, each piece is one-eighth of the apple.

11. A

The answer to this question can be found in the second sentence in step 4. After the apple slices are placed in the oven, they need to be turned once every hour so that the slices dry evenly.

12. B

Ovens are used for cooking. In order to cook things, ovens must be hot. When something is put into or taken out of an oven, hands should be covered with oven mitts to protect them from getting burned.

13. A

Tasting the apple slices will not show if there is any moisture left in the slices because a mouth contains moisture. Since the apple slices are turned when they are cooked, this is not the way to test if they are done. When the apples are removed from the oven, they must first be cooled. To test and see if the apple slices are dry, they need to be squeezed. The answer is given in the second sentence in step 5: "Test the slices by squeezing them."

Squiggle and the Giant

14. B

Squiggle's grandfather must have described pavement to Squiggle as being hard and rough because in the first paragraph, when Squiggle ends up on a hard, rough surface, he connects the experience to his grandfather's warning about pavement.

15. C

The giant came along after the puddle was gone. If there was a hole in the pavement and the water was running into it, the water would not have gathered and created a puddle for Squiggle to play in. If the puddle had filled with mud, Squiggle would have been covered with mud and dirty water, but he was not. The second paragraph says the rain stopped falling, the air got warmer, and the puddles got smaller and smaller. If the air got warmer and then the puddles started to shrink, the warmth of the air is the most likely reason that the puddles were shrinking.

16. D

The pavement was hard when Squiggle began to move on it. He was able to move onto the pavement because the rain made his skin wet and slippery. When the rain stopped falling and the puddle dried up, Squiggle's skin became dry. Squiggle could not move after the puddle had dried up because his skin was too dry.

17. D

The first sentence in the fourth paragraph says, "The ground began to tremble." The word "tremble" means that the ground moved or shook. The weight of the giant made the pavement tremble. Squiggle knew that a giant was coming because he felt the ground move.

18. A

Squiggle learned a lesson from his experience. He learned that pavement is dangerous because he cannot burrow into it. He also learned that puddles are fun to play in, but they do not stay forever. He will now take his grandfather's warning seriously. The next time Squiggle feels pavement, he will likely remember his scary experience and wiggle back to the soft earth where he can burrow if he needs or wants to.

Rock Read

19. A

The words "years passed" could mean two or more years, so it is not the best choice. "One day" and "once been" could also be used to tell of a time in the past, but they do not give us any strong clues about how long ago. People use the words "long ago" to tell of a time long past. Dinosaurs have not been on Earth for a very long time, so the best choice is "Long ago."

20. A

This question asks which dinosaur died <u>here</u>. The Tyrannosaurus or the Edmontonsaurus cannot be the correct answer because they are not part of the story "Rock Read." Find the word "here" in the story passage. The diagram that comes just before it represents the Stegosaurus. The dinosaur that died <u>here</u> is the Stegosaurus.

21. A

This question asks what lived in the lake. The forest is not the correct choice. The forest grew many years after the volcano erupted near where the lake was. The third sentence in this story implies that the Teratosaurus and the Stegosaurus had once lived on the land where the lake formed millions of years later. This same sentence tells what did live in the lake; turtles lived in the lake.

22. D

To figure out the answer to this question, pay close attention to the order in which things happened (i.e., before/after). Turtles were living in the lake before the volcano erupted. The passage says that the forest grew *by* the lake. The use of the word "by" means that after the volcanic eruption, the lake was still there, but this is wrong because the lake no longer existed. The forest grew right where the lake used to be. Dinosaurs left their footprints millions of years before the volcanic eruption. The fourth sentence of the story gives the answer. After the picture of the volcano erupting, the sentence shows the picture of the lake and says that it was filled "with lava and ash." After the volcano erupted, the lake filled with lava and ash.

23. B

The words *fossil* and *mountain* are not found in the story. Therefore, they cannot be the right choices. The volcano was there at the same time that the lake was, so that answer cannot be correct. The words "after a long time" are used in the question and in the story. Locate these words to find the answer. These words are located in the last sentence. According to the picture, the forest grew where the lake had once been.

SECTION B

The Wing Shop

24. B

Matthew met Lucy when he went to buy a pair of wings from her grandfather's store. Matthew does not know Lucy's grandfather and did not offer to help find him. In the fifth paragraph, Matthew asks Lucy if she has a pair of wings that will get him "back to Main Street."

25. C

Lucy frowns because she is unsure of which wings to sell Matthew to get him back to Main Street. Lucy's grandfather owns the store. She is just watching the store for her grandfather while he is away. Matthew picked out his own set of wings because Lucy does not know much about the wings.

26. B

Matthew was worried because he was flying far off of the ground high above the city's buildings. The question asks why Matthew was worried that he was "flying in the wrong direction." The reason he was worried that he was flying in the wrong direction was that he was flying toward the harbour instead of toward Main Street.

27. C

Matthew soared high up in the sky. Penguins do not fly and chickens flap their wings and are only able to move small distances in the air. Neither penguins nor chickens are able to soar high above city buildings. Crows and sea gulls are both able to fly high up in the sky. Crows are black. Matthew's grey and white wings were taking him to the harbour. Sea gulls are known to fly around harbours, and their wings are grey and white. So, the wings Matthew put on were probably those of a sea gull.

Giants of the Forest

28. C

The story tells of how big redwood trees are. The word "barely" means that the people could *hardly* reach round the tree. This word is used to show how very big the tree is. It is so big that the six people were just able to hold hands around it.

29. D

We know that plants need sunlight to grow. The redwood trees are very big. Few plants grow around redwood trees "because redwood branches keep the sunlight from getting to the forest floor." The ground around them is shaded.

30. B

Redwoods are big around, very tall, and grow near the Pacific Ocean. However, the reason that they live for so long is given in the first sentence of the last paragraph. Redwoods live to be some of world's oldest things because "redwoods are so healthy."

My Toboggan and I Carve Winter

31. A

The words "RACE" and "WHOMP" do not describe snow or tell who the winner is. If only the word "WHOMP" were capitalized, answer B could be correct because "WHOMP" is a noise; however, there are two words that are capitalized. When people "RACE," their hearts beat very fast because it is exciting. The poem describes the toboggan racing down the hill at a very high speed and then "WHOMP." The word "WHOMP" describes the toboggan stopping very suddenly because of a bump. Tumbling off the toboggan unexpectedly would be somewhat scary, but exciting as well. These two words are probably capitalized to show an exciting action.

32. D

The two lines before the underlined words give clues to what the words refer to. The poet is writing about racing down the hill "faster and faster." These two words tell you that the poet uses the words "whipping the wind" to describe a toboggan going really fast.

33. D

Racing down a hill on a toboggan is very exciting. The words "nearing full flight" mean that the toboggan is almost at its top speed. The child in the poem would probably not be feeling sad, bored, or lonely at this exciting time. The child would probably be feeling thrilled.

34. D

The first three choices are incorrect. The child moves over the "powdery snow" with the toboggan, goes fast enough to whip the wind, and circles around the shadows of trees, but none of these things cause the child to fall off the toboggan. The child tumbles after hitting "a lurking bump."

35. A

"My Friends and I" would not be an appropriate title because the child is tobogganing alone. The poet uses the word "we" for the child and the toboggan. The child is tobogganing over powdery snow and the poet does mention "freezing snow," but these are not key ideas to the poem. Another good title for this poem is "Winter Fun" because the child is having fun tobogganing and enjoying the winter weather.

The Watcher

36. A

George liked to watch everything. The story says that he loved to watch shoppers at the mall and birds at the bird feeder. Since birds at the bird feeder is not included as one of the answers, George liked to watch shoppers at the mall.

37. B

When George saw Sarah, he could tell that she was choking. To see someone choking would probably be scary. When he saw her choking, he yelled her name. A person who is proud or sick would probably not yell. He told Dan that he had seen a safety show and knew he had to stay calm and not be excited.

38. C

The story takes place "One Monday at noon." Usually, children are at school on a weekday. Since the school nurse helped Sarah when she was choking, the story takes place in a school.

39. B

George was sitting, and when he saw the problem, he "sprang out of his seat." A person who sees an emergency must react quickly. Of the four choices, "jumped quickly" shows that he was getting up to help Sarah.

40. A

A lesson is something we learn from one situation that can be used at other times. George was able to help Sarah because he was watching what people were doing. The lesson in this story is that by watching, people can help each other.

2001 PROVINCIAL ACHIEVEMENT TEST

English Language Arts

PART B: READING

Some readings, questions, and solutions are common to both the 2000 and 2001 provincial achievement tests, and will not be repeated here.

Description

This test has 2 sections: Section A has 5 selections and 23 questions.

Section B has 4 selections and 17 questions.

You have 60 minutes to complete this test. Your teacher will give you a break between Section A and Section B. You may take up to 30 extra minutes to complete this test.

Instructions to Students

- You will need a pencil and eraser. Use **ONLY** an HB pencil.
- Read each selection carefully. Read each question carefully.
- You may underline any key words in the passage or question that may help you.
- Choose the **BEST** or **CORRECT** answer.
- Mark your answer in this booklet by filling in the circle next to your answer. Look at the example below to see how to mark your answer.
- If you want to change an answer, erase your first mark **COMPLETELY**.
- When you are finished the test, go back and **CHECK** that you did each question. You may want to read each selection again.

Example Question

Rex is a big dinosaur. He is taller than a giraffe. Rex is as tall as a house!

1. **Rex is a**

   Ⓐ pet

   Ⓑ bird

   Ⓒ giraffe

 dinosaur

SECTION A

I. Read the following story and answer questions 1 to 5.

from **Tales of a Fourth Grade Nothing**

My bedroom door was open. . . . I ran to my dresser to check Dribble. He wasn't there! …

I got really scared. I thought, *Maybe he died while I was at school and I didn't know about it.* So I rushed into the kitchen and hollered, "Mom . . . where's Dribble?" My mother was baking something. My brother sat on the kitchen floor, banging pots and pans together. "Be quiet!" I yelled at Fudge. "I can't hear anything with all that noise."

"What did you say, Peter?" my mother asked me.

"I said I can't find Dribble. Where is he?"

"You mean he's not in his bowl?" my mother asked.

I shook my head.

"Oh dear!" my mother said. "I hope he's not crawling around somewhere. You know I don't like the way he smells. I'm going to have a look in the bedrooms. You check in here, Peter."

…looked at my brother. He was smiling. "Fudge, do you know where Dribble is?" I asked calmly.

Fudge kept smiling.

"Did you take him? Did you, Fudge?" I asked not so calmly.

Fudge giggled and covered his mouth with his hands.

I yelled. "Where is he? What did you do with my turtle?"

…I tried to speak softly. "Now tell me where Dribble is. Come on, Fudge … please."

Fudge looked up at me. "In tummy," he said.

"What do you mean, in tummy?" I asked, narrowing my eyes.

"Dribble in tummy!" he repeated.

"What tummy?" I shouted at my brother.

"This one," Fudge said, rubbing his stomach. "Dribble in this tummy!

Right here!"

Judy Blume

1. **The first thing Peter did after he got home was**

    Ⓐ   open his bedroom door

    Ⓑ   check on his pet turtle

    Ⓒ   shout at his mother

    Ⓓ   change his clothes

2. **Peter was afraid that his pet turtle**

    Ⓐ   was dead

    Ⓑ   had been stolen

    Ⓒ   was lost in the bedroom

    Ⓓ   had climbed out of its bowl

3. **Peter's mother wanted to find Dribble because she**

    Ⓐ   was afraid of him

    Ⓑ   thought he smelled bad

    Ⓒ   had to get back to her baking

    Ⓓ   was worried he would go outside

4. **When Peter first asked his brother about the missing turtle, Fudge**

   Ⓐ ran to his dresser

   Ⓑ rubbed his tummy

   Ⓒ smiled and giggled

   Ⓓ banged the pots and pans

5. **Fudge was MOST LIKELY smiling because he**

   Ⓐ was having fun with the pots and pans

   Ⓑ liked being with his mom and brother

   Ⓒ knew something no one else knew

   Ⓓ was playing and giggling

II. Read the following poem and answer questions 6 to 9.

Daddy Fell into the Pond

Everyone grumbled. The sky was gray.
We had nothing to do and nothing to say.
We were nearing the end of a dismal day,
And there seemed to be nothing beyond,
    <u>THEN</u>
    Daddy fell into the pond!

And everyone's face grew merry and bright,
And Timothy danced for sheer delight.
"Give me the camera, quick, oh quick!
He's crawling out of the duckweed." <u>*Click*</u>*!*

Then the gardener suddenly slapped his knee,
And doubled up, shaking silently,
And the ducks all quacked as if they were daft
And it sounded as if the old drake laughed.

Oh, there wasn't a thing that didn't respond
    WHEN
    Daddy fell into the pond!

Alfred Noyes

6. **Before Daddy fell into the pond, everyone was**

Ⓐ relaxing

Ⓑ playing

Ⓒ bored

Ⓓ tired

7. **The author of the poem PROBABLY wrote <u>THEN</u> in capital letters to show that**

Ⓐ what happened was a surprise

Ⓑ Daddy made a loud noise

Ⓒ it was time to go home

Ⓓ it rhymes with WHEN

8. **After crawling out of the pond, Daddy MOST LIKELY felt**

Ⓐ merry

Ⓑ dismal

Ⓒ delighted

Ⓓ embarrassed

9. **The underlined word *Click* helps the reader to hear**

Ⓐ Timothy taking a picture

Ⓑ Daddy splashing the water

Ⓒ the gardener slapping his knee

Ⓓ the ducks splashing in the pond

III. **Read the following story and answer questions 10 to 13.**

from **Two Bad Ants**

The excerpt from *Two Bad Ants* by Chris Van Allsburg, and questions 10 to 13, are not reprinted here, as they are a repeat of the 2000 Provincial Achievement Test included in this resource.

IV. **Read the following recipe and answer questions 14 to 18.**

from **A Pioneer Story**

The excerpt from *A Pioneer Story* by Barbara Greenwood, and questions 14 to 18, are not reprinted here, as they are a repeat of the 2000 Provincial Achievement Test included in this resource.

V. Read the following story and answer questions 19 to 23.

from **The Dust Bowl**

On Sunday morning, the wind blew outside the kitchen window. Matthew wiped the dust from his cereal bowl. He was used to removing the fine coating from everything in the house. It was almost as dusty inside as out…

When his father and his grandpa joined him at the table, they didn't say much, but he knew what they were thinking. Finally, he blurted out, "We aren't going to sell the farm, are we?"

His father set down his coffee mug and looked at Matthew's grandpa. "How much longer can we last, Pop?"

"As long as it takes," Grandpa answered.

"But the crops won't make it this year," his father <u>snapped</u>. "Without rain, there'll be no grain. Without grain, there'll be no money."

Matthew said nothing. His grandpa stood up and walked over to the window. "The rain will come. The wheat will grow. It's not as bad as the last <u>drought</u>."

Matthew's father pushed his chair back angrily and went outside. He began to work in the small garden below the porch. . . .

Matthew went outside. . . . "Will we have to sell the farm, Dad?"

Grandpa called out through the screen door, "The rain will come. If not this year, then next year. We can <u>hang on</u>."

David Booth

19. **The inside of the house was dirty because the**

Ⓐ screen door was left open

Ⓑ family was busy farming

Ⓒ wind blew in the dust

Ⓓ the dishes needed washing

20. **Matthew MOST LIKELY knew what his dad and grandpa were thinking by the**

Ⓐ way they were acting

Ⓑ sound of their voices

Ⓒ way they were dressed

Ⓓ questions they were asking

21. **The author used the word <u>snapped</u> to show that Matthew's father was**

Ⓐ tired

Ⓑ angry

Ⓒ hungry

Ⓓ thinking

22. During a <u>drought</u>, the weather is

    Ⓐ   cold and cloudy

    Ⓑ   warm and clear

    Ⓒ   wet and windy

    Ⓓ   hot and dry

23. Grandpa believed they could <u>hang on</u> to the farm because he

    Ⓐ   was a good farmer

    Ⓑ   had planted a big crop

    Ⓒ   got a good price for the wheat

    Ⓓ   had lived through hard times before

SECTION B

VI. Read the following story and answer questions 24 to 28.

from **Squiggle and the Giant**

The excerpt from *Squiggle and the Giant* by D.A. Woodliff, and questions 24 to 28, are not reprinted here, as they are a repeat of the 2000 Provincial Achievement Test included in this resource.

VII. Read the following story and answer questions 29 to 32.

from **The Wing Shop**

The excerpt from *The Wing Shop* by Elvira Woodruff, and questions 29 to 32, are not reprinted here, as they are a repeat of the 2000 Provincial Achievement Test included in this resource.

VIII. Read the following information and answer questions 33 to 35.

from **Giants of the Forest**

The excerpt from *Giants of the Forest* from *The Homework Booklet*, and questions 33 to 35, are not reprinted here, as they are a repeat of the 2000 Provincial Achievement Test included in this resource.

IX. Read the following information and answer questions 36 to 40.

Ghost Bears

Have you ever heard of the Ghost Bear? They are very rare. Their coats are light-coloured but they are not Polar Bears. They actually belong to the family of black bears and are small in size.

Ghost Bears live in northern rainforests. They love to eat salmon but also eat plants, insects, nuts, berries and honey. The first person to study Ghost Bears was Francis Kermode that is why they are called Kermode (Kur-mo-dee).

The native people on Canada's west coast tell stories about the shy Ghost Bear. The stories explain how Raven the Creator gave the Ghost Bear special powers. Raven did this to give a reminder of what the world was like when it was covered in ice and snow.

36. The underlined word <u>rare</u> means

Ⓐ beautiful

Ⓑ unusual

Ⓒ small

Ⓓ shy

37. You are lucky if you see a Ghost Bear because

Ⓐ the fur of a Ghost Bear is the colour of snow

Ⓑ Ghost Bears only come out at night

Ⓒ there are so few Ghost Bears

Ⓓ a Ghost Bear is so small

38. Ghost Bears live

Ⓐ in the far north

Ⓑ near snow and ice

Ⓒ all over the country

Ⓓ in northern rainforests

39. Ghost Bears and Polar Bears

    Ⓐ   are the same size

    Ⓑ   eat the same food

    Ⓒ   are the same colour

    Ⓓ   live in the same area

40. Francis Kermode was the first person to

    Ⓐ   see Ghost Bears

    Ⓑ   study Ghost Bears

    Ⓒ   tell stories about Ghost Bears

    Ⓓ   give special powers to Ghost Bears

ANSWERS AND SOLUTIONS
2001 PROVINCIAL ACHIEVEMENT TEST

1. B	9. A	17. B	25. C	33. C
2. A	10. D	18. A	26. D	34. D
3. B	11. D	19. A	27. D	35. B
4. C	12. C	20. A	28. A	36. B
5. C	13. A	21. B	29. B	37. C
6. C	14. B	22. D	30. C	38. D
7. A	15. C	23. D	31. A	39. C
8. D	16. A	24. B	32. C	40. B

Some readings, questions, and solutions are common to both the 2000 and 2001 provincial achievement tests. The common solutions have been omitted from this section.

SECTION A

Tales of a Fourth Grade Nothing

1. B

The first thing Peter did when he got home was check on his turtle. The door to his room was already open. He did not change his clothes. Peter shouted at his mother after he checked on the turtle because he needed to ask her where Dribble the turtle was.

2. A

The answer to this question is found in the second sentence in the second paragraph. Peter thought, *"Maybe he died while I was at school."* Peter was afraid that his pet turtle had died.

3. B

Peter's mother was not afraid of Dribble nor was she worried that he would go outside. Finding Dribble had nothing to do with her baking. Peter's mother wanted to find Dribble because she did not "'like the way that he smells.'"

4. C

Fudge never ran to a dresser. He did bang pots and pans, rub his tummy, and smile and giggle. It is important to figure out the order in which Fudge did these things. The question asks about the **first** thing Fudge did when Peter asked him about the turtle. Fudge was banging pots and pans before Peter asked him about Dribble. Fudge smiled and giggled right after Peter asked him about Fudge. After that, he rubbed his tummy.

5. C

Fudge could have been smiling for any of the reasons given in the answers. Neither Peter nor his mom knew where Dribble was, so they were looking for Dribble. Fudge just sat smiling at Peter. He was most likely smiling because Peter was asking a question that only Fudge knew the answer to. Fudge knew something that no one else knew.

Daddy Fell Into The Pond

6. C

The poem starts off by describing a gloomy day. The answer to the question can be found in the second line. People use the word "bored" when they feel that they have "nothing to do and nothing to say." Before Daddy fell into the pond, everyone was bored.

7. A

The mood of the poem is quite glum up to the point where Daddy fell into the pond. Daddy most likely made a loud noise when he fell into the pond, but the word "THEN" was probably used to show that the action of falling in was unexpected. The word "THEN" is used to show that what happened was a surprise.

8. D

When Daddy fell into the pond, everyone's mood changed. Everyone was laughing at Daddy. His fall into the pond made other people feel merry and delighted. Daddy could be feeling dismal, but being laughed at usually makes people embarrassed. After crawling out of the pond, Daddy most likely felt embarrassed.

9. A

The answer cannot be the gardener slapping his knee because the gardener did that after the "*Click*." The sound "*Click*" would not be used as a sound of splashing water. The third line in the second stanza says, "'Give me the camera, quick, oh quick!'" This line tells us that Timothy is getting a camera. Cameras make a "click" noise when a picture is being taken. The "*Click*" helps the reader to hear the noise the camera makes as Timothy takes Daddy's picture.

Two Bad Ants

For detailed solutions to questions 10 to 13, please see the Answers and Solutions section for the 2000 Provincial Achievement Test.

A Pioneer Story

For detailed solutions to questions 14 to 18, please see the Answers and Solutions section for the 2000 Provincial Achievement Test.

The Dust Bowl

19. C

Two clues are given for the answer to this question: in the first and last lines of the first paragraph. The first line mentions the wind blowing, and the last line compares the dust outside with the dust inside. Putting these ideas together gives the answer. The inside of the house was dirty because the wind blew in the dust.

20. A

Just before Matthew asks about selling the farm, the story says that his father and grandfather did not say much; therefore, the "sound of their voices" and "questions they were asking" are probably not correct. It does not make sense for someone to be able to tell what other people are thinking by the way they are dressed. Often, when people do not talk, they are thinking seriously about something or they are upset. Matthew most likely knew what his father and grandfather were thinking by the way they were acting.

21. B

People may "snap" when they are hungry, tired, or interrupted from deep thought; however, Matthew's dad snapped because he was angry. We know this by reading the discussion between Matthew's dad and his grandfather.
The grandfather wants to keep the farm and is willing to wait until the rain comes, while Matthew's father disagrees. He does not think waiting is a good idea. Matthew's father was angry.

22. D

Matthew's father and grandfather are talking about the lack of rain, so we know that the word "drought" does not mean wet and windy. People do not farm in the months when the weather is cold. While the weather may have been "warm and clear," the weather in a drought is hot, not warm. Since there has not been any rain for quite some time, Matthew's father and grandfather are worried. If there has not been any rain for a long time, the weather is very dry. The heat without rain would further damage the crops. A drought is when the weather is hot and dry.

23. D

Even if Matthew's grandfather was a good farmer or had planted a big crop, the lack of rain and the hot temperature would not allow the crop to grow. He could not get a good price for wheat because the crops were suffering and there would be no wheat to sell. Matthew's grandfather believed they could hang on to the farm because he had lived through hard times before. We know this by reading the last sentence in the sixth paragraph, "'It's not as bad as the last drought.'" The word "last" tells that something like this has happened before.

Section B

Squiggle and the Giant

For detailed solutions to questions 24 to 28, please see the Answers and Solutions section for the 2000 Provincial Achievement Test.

The Wing Shop

For detailed solutions to questions 29 to 32, please see the Answers and Solutions section for the 2000 Provincial Achievement Test.

Giants of the Forest

For detailed solutions to questions 33 to 35, please see the Answers and Solutions section for the 2000 Provincial Achievement Test.

Ghost Bears

36. B

The word "lucky" in the first line gives a clue to the meaning of the word "rare." If someone is lucky to see a Ghost Bear, it is likely that very few people ever see one. The bear must be unusual. It is stated in the second paragraph that only "One out of every ten bears" is a Ghost Bear. The word "rare" means *unusual*.

37. C

The story does not mention that Ghost Bears only come out at night. Ghost Bears do have fur the colour of snow and they are small, but these are not the reasons you would be lucky to see one. You are lucky to see one because only "One out of every ten bears" is a Ghost Bear. This means that you would be lucky to see one because there are so few Ghost Bears.

38. D

Ghost Bears do not live all over the country. They do not live near snow and ice in the north. The answer to this question can be found in the first paragraph: "Ghost Bears live in the northern rainforests."

39. C

Ghost Bears are smaller than Polar Bears. Ghost Bears eat "berries, honey, plants, nuts, insects." Polar Bears could not eat these things because there is snow where they live. Plants do not grow in snow. Since bees cannot live in the cold, there would not be any bees to make the honey. Sometimes, people think that Ghost Bears are Polar Bears because they are the same colour—white.

40. B

We do not know if Francis Kermode was the first person to see a Ghost Bear or tell stories about Ghost Bears. We do know that people believe that Raven, not Francis Kermode, gave Ghost Bears special powers. We also know by reading the last line in the second paragraph that Francis Kermode was the first person to study Ghost Bears.

GLOSSARY OF TERMS

Adjective	Describes a noun or pronoun The *red* car raced down the *narrow* street. (The adjectives "red" and "narrow" describe the nouns "car" and "street")
Adverb	Describes a verb, an adjective, or another adverb. *Yesterday*, the red car raced *quickly* down the narrow street. (The adverbs "yesterday" and "quickly" describe the verb "raced" by answering when and how the red car raced)
Affix	Element added to a root word to form a new word (see *prefix* and *suffix* below) *un*– (prefix) + *forget* (root) + *–able* (suffix) = unforgettable (*un*– and *–able* are both affixes)
Apostrophe	A punctuation mark used to show belonging The *boy's* bike is fast.
Audience	The people for whom the work is written Other students, teacher, political leaders, etc.
Capital Letters	These letters are used mostly at the beginning of a sentence, for the pronoun "I", for the first letter of important words in a title, and to begin names of people, places, and things.
Comma	A punctuation mark used between words or expressions that are for example, in a list or a series I ate chicken, fries, and carrots for lunch today.
Compound Sentence	A sentence that is made up of two sentences joined together by words such as "and", "but," "or," or "yet"
Dictionary	Will give you the meaning of words and often explains how to pronounce and use them correctly.
Exclamation Mark	A punctuation mark used at the end of sentence that shows excitement What a surprise!
Form for Writing	The manner of style of arranging the written work Personal journal, friendly letter, narrative, poetry, etc.
Glossary	Usually found at the back of a book, most often in a non-fiction book. It lists and explains words about the particular subject area of the book

Graphic Organizer	A visual way to organize information chronological sequence, comparison/contrast chart, Venn diagram, concept web, episode web, generalization/principle, etc.
Homonym	Words that sound the same but are not spelled the same and have different meanings *there* (in that place); *their* (belonging to them)
Inflection	Different pronunciations of words that are spelled the same *tear* (droplet of water shed from the eye) *tear* (rip)
Kinds of Sentences	Declarative (makes a statement) I am hungry. Interrogative (asks a question) Are you hungry? Imperative (commands or orders) Have some food. Exclamatory (shows excitement) That was delicious!
Main Idea	The explanation of what a reading passage is about
Noun	Person(s), place(s), or thing(s) teachers, London, park
Paragraph	A group of sentences that tell about a topic
Period	A punctuation mark used at the end of sentence that tells something or makes a command The field trip was very exciting.
Plural	More than one. *bus* (singular); *buses* (plural)
Prefix	A group of letters that is added to the beginning of a root word *turn* (root word); *return* (added prefix "re")
Pronoun	A word that takes the place of a noun. Olivia skipped all the way to school. *She* skipped all the way to school. (The noun "Olivia" is replaced with the pronoun "she")

Proper Noun	The name of a specific person, place, or thing *John Smith*, *Toronto*, the *Canadian Museum of Nature*
Purpose	The reason the author has created the written work to inform, to explain, to entertain, to impress, to convince, etc.
Question Mark	A punctuation mark used at the end of a sentence that asks something Are you going to the movie tonight?
Root	Carries the basic meaning of a word *Rewriting*; root word = *write*
Simple Sentence	A sentence that has a person, place, or thing doing something
Suffix	A group of letters that is added to the end of a root word *jump* (root word) *jumped* (added suffix "ed")
Supporting Details	The sentences and phrases that give details and examples that support the main idea
Syllable	Words are made up of one or more syllables, each containing a sounded vowel. The word "Canadian" has 4 syllables: Ca/na/di/an
Table of Contents	Found at the front of a book and it provides the chapters or divisions in a book, in order from first to last
Thesaurus	Is a special dictionary of synonyms and often, antonyms that are arranged in alphabetical order
Topic	The subject or theme of a specific written work
Verb	Words that tell us actions The car *raced* down the street. (*Raced* is the verb)
Verb Tense	Tells us whether the action happened in the past (past tense), is happening in the present (present tense), or will happen in the future (future tense). I *rode* my bike to school. (Past tense verb – *rode*) I *ride* my bike to school (present tense verb – *ride*) I *will ride* my bike to school (future tense verb – *will ride*)
Words and Expressions	Specific terms used in your own writing that help the reader to understand exactly what you mean, describe things clearly, and help the reader see, feel, hear, smell, or taste as if the reader were in the story

CREDITS

Every effort has been made to provide proper acknowledgment of the original sources and to comply with copyright law. However, some attempts to establish original copyright ownership may have been unsuccessful. If copyright ownership can be identified, please notify Castle Rock Research Corporation so that appropriate corrective action can be taken.

Excerpt from TWO BAD ANTS by Chris Van Allsburg. Copyright © 1988 by Chris Van Allsburg. Reprinted by permission of Houghton Mifflin Harcourt Publishing Company. All rights reserved.

"Drying Apples", a selection from *A Pioneer Story*, written by Barbara Greenwood is used by permission of Kids Can Press Ltd., Toronto. Text © 1994 Barbara Greenwood

Excerpt from "Squiggle and the Giant" by D.A. Woodliff, Copyright © 1990 by Highlights for Children, Inc., Columbus, Ohio

"The Wing Shop" by Elvira Woodruff. Text copyright © 1991 by Elvira Woodruff. Illustrations copyright © 1991 by Stephen Gammell. All rights reserved. Reprinted from THE WING SHOP by permission of Holiday House, Inc.

"My Toboggan and I Carve Winter" by Jane Wadley

Illustration from Til All the Stars Have Fallen, selected by David Booth and illustrated by Kady MacDonald Denton used by permission of Kids Can Press Ltd., Toronto. Illustration © 1989 by Kady MacDonald Denton.

"The Watcher" by Brenda Silsbe. © 1995 by Brenda Silsbe. Reprinted by permission of the publisher, Annick Press

From TALES OF A FOURTH GRADE NOTHING by Judy Blume, copyright © 1972 by Judy Blume. Illustrations copyright © 1972 by E.P. Dutton. Used by permission of Dutton Children's Books, A Division of Penguin Young Readers Group, A Member of Penguin Group (USA) Inc., 345 Hudson Street, New York, NY 10014. All rights reserved

"Daddy Fell into the Pond" by Alfred Noyes

Material from "The Dust Bowl", written by David Booth. Used by permission of Kids Can press Ltd., Toronto. Text © 1996 by David Booth

"Ghost Bears" by Marilyn Baillie. ChickaDEE vol. 20, no. 7, October 1998.

Clipart ©2013 Clipart.com, a division of Getty Images.

NOTES

BOOK ORDERING INFORMATION
ELEMENTARY and JUNIOR HIGH TITLES

Castle Rock Research offers the following resources to support Alberta students. You can order any of these materials online at:

www.castlerockresearch.com/store

SOLARO - Online Learning		The KEY	SNAP	Prob Solved	Class Notes
$29.95 ea.*		$29.95 ea.*	$29.95 ea.*	$19.95 ea.*	$19.95 ea.*
English Language Arts 9	English Language Arts 6	English Language Arts 9	Science 9	Science 9	Science 9
English Language Arts 8	English Language Arts 5	English Language Arts 6	Mathematics 9	Mathematics 9	Mathematics 9
English Language Arts 7	English Language Arts 4	English Language Arts 3	Mathematics 8	Mathematics 8	Mathematics 8
Mathematics 9	English Language Arts 3	Mathematics 9	Mathematics 7	Mathematics 7	Mathematics 7
Mathematics 8	Mathematics 6	Mathematics 8	Mathematics 6		
Mathematics 7	Mathematics 5	Mathematics 7	Mathematics 5		
Science 9	Mathematics 4	Mathematics 6	Mathematics 4		
Science 8	Mathematics 3	Mathematics 4	Mathematics 3		
Science 7	Science 6	Mathematics 3			
Social Studies 9	Science 5	Science 9			
Social Studies 6	Science 4	Science 6			
	Science 3	Social Studies 9			
		Social Studies 6			

Prices do not include taxes or shipping.

Study online using **SOLARO,** with access to multiple courses available by either a monthly or an annual subscription.

The KEY Study Guide is specifically designed to assist students in preparing for unit tests, final exams, and provincial examinations.

The **Student Notes and Problems (SNAP) Workbook** contains complete explanations of curriculum concepts, examples, and exercise questions.

The **Problem Solved** contains exercise questions and complete solutions.

The **Class Notes** contains complete explanations of curriculum concepts.

If you would like to order Castle Rock resources for your school, please visit our school ordering page:
www.castlerockresearch.com/school-orders/